TAKING OUR OWN SIDE

AND OTHER ESSAYS

by

MICHAEL J. POLIGNANO

EDITED BY GREG JOHNSON

Counter-Currents Publishing Ltd.
San Francisco
2010

Cover image:
Peter Paul Rubens
The Battle of Anghiari, 1603
(Copy of a lost work of Leonardo da Vinci, 1505)
Musée du Louvre

Cover design by
Greg Johnson & Michael J. Polignano

Published in the United States by
COUNTER-CURRENTS PUBLISHING LTD.
P.O. Box 22638
San Francisco, CA 94122
USA
http://www.counter-currents.com/

Hardcover Edition:
ISBN: 978-1-935965-04-6

Paperback Edition:
ISBN: 978-1-935965-05-3

CONTENTS

FOREWORD

KEVIN MACDONALD

The triumph of the cultural left is an ongoing disaster to America and every other Western country. The result is stultifying intellectual conformity in all the elite institutions of society, particularly the educational system. All levels of the educational system are rigorously policed to ensure ideological conformity, with the result that college graduates — especially college graduates — emerge zombie-like, mouthing politically correct platitudes they heard from their brilliant professors, mindlessly looking forward to an impossible future of racial harmony where the White minority adapts seamlessly and joyously to life among their non-White brothers.

Michael Polignano somehow managed to overcome all that. And what's really amazing is that he did it while still a college student. Overcoming the propaganda is a remarkable achievement at any age, but is especially difficult for young people. Not only have they been subjected to this massive propaganda assault since kindergarten, they have to overcome the natural human proclivity to conformity that is especially strong among young people. I am ashamed to say that I was hopelessly conformist in college and grad school. Even after becoming ever more disenchanted with the left (I was happy Reagan was elected), I couldn't really get out of the narrow confines of the political mainstream.

Mike Polignano gets it. This is about racial survival: "A proposed moral principle cannot conflict with the survival of the race." He is a biologist by training, and it shows. He has a clear understanding of group interests:

> The reality is: The races are at war with one another. The different human races are distinct subspecies, with distinct temperaments and talents, some of which conflict dramatically. It is an iron biological law that when two distinct

subspecies try to occupy the same ecological niche in the same geographical region, there will be group conflict. . . . But since we're rational creatures, humans also have [another] option: voluntary separation. This last option preserves racial uniqueness and eliminates interracial competition, allowing each race to shape the course of its own future.

Mike Polignano rejects White guilt. We have to develop a sense of urgency to reverse the tide that is swelling against us: "In this time of racial peril, the highest and noblest thing any of us can do is work together to ensure the survival and flourishing of the white race, so it can give birth to new Leonardos and Newtons and Teslas." I couldn't agree more.

Multiculturalism then becomes not a source of strength, but the ideology of White dispossession—nothing more than "an attempt to replace White cultures with non-White cultures—or, more precisely, with fantasies, lies, and sanitized half-truths about non-White cultures designed to make them seem spiritually and morally superior."

And as he notes, "Social ostracism is a small thing to risk considering what's at stake." Indeed, he correctly sees Whites as "too polite, too concerned to accommodate and demonstrate goodwill to non-White invaders." It is a politeness fueled at least partly by the desire not to be ostracized, not to take views that oppose what all the "smart people" in the universities and the elite media believe. Going against it takes a lot of intellectual confidence and a very thick skin.

Mike Polignano is a race realist in every sense of the word. Although he sees Whites as having made unique and irreplaceable contributions to civilization, he also advocates eugenics. The White gene pool could be improved by providing incentives for the best and the brightest to have children.

Eugenics is an idea that that was once championed by progressive thinkers of all political persuasions but has fallen into disfavor because the contemporary left rejects any acknowledgment that genes influence important behaviors like IQ—despite the overwhelming evidence from research. Nowadays, there is an automatic, knee-jerk accusation of Nazi sympathies whenever eugenics is mentioned. But the research is quite clear that genetic influences explain most of the variation in intelligence. And that implies that eugenic breeding practices would indeed be effective.

Polignano is also a race realist when it comes to race differences in IQ. The left quickly noticed that civil rights laws and an equal playing field did not result in equal outcomes. The result has been affirmative action designed to magically create a non-White elite with all the same skills as the people they are displacing accompanied by massive propaganda featuring brilliant Blacks and stupid Whites. The result is:

> a Potemkin village increasingly populated by non-Whites who, regardless of their real merits, have been promoted a rung or two above those merits because of their race. Television and the movies portray a fantasy world filled with dumb blondes and Black doctors, lawyers, judges, inventors, and computer geniuses. But behind the façade hides a vast, squalid reality of false promises, false hopes, and outright falsehoods about race — all premised on the refusal to accept racial inequality as a natural fact.

Polignano is also a realist when it comes to Jewish influence. He has a hilarious spoof on the "Differently Intelligent" and the "National Association for the Advancement of Retarded People" where all the advocates for these unfortunate souls are highly accomplished people with obvious Jewish names:

> The NAARP was founded and staffed by the law firm of Wiesel, Wiener, Liehr, Ratner, and Cohen (Ari Wiesel, JD, Harvard, SAT 1560; Barry Wiener, JD, Yale, SAT 1470; Aaron Liehr, JD, Harvard, SAT 1510; Shulamith Ratner, JD, Harvard, SAT 1520; and Adam Cohen, JD, Yale, SAT 1420). (Mr. Wiener returned to private practice in 1999 after the passage of the Equalization of Opportunity Act and has won multi-billion dollar settlements in class action suits on behalf of DI individuals.)

Although this is satire, it points to a real issue: Very intelligent Jews from the very best schools have used their abilities to engineer the Potemkin village of Black and Latino accomplishment — not to mention altering the law on Church-State relations and promoting the "rights" of immigrants, legal and illegal: the Jewish elite hostile to the traditional White majority of America.

Polignano also points to two key traits of Jews that make them such formidable enemies to White America and the West: (1) Their powerful sense of collectivism — that Jews have a strong sense of Jewish communal interest and have a remarkable agreement on the basic issues they see as benefiting Jews — particularly issues such as immigration and multiculturalism in the US, and support for Israel as an ethnically exclusive Jewish state. (2) The Jewish hatred of Christianity "which over the centuries has given rise to terrible persecutions whenever Jews have gained political power." This is exactly right.

One very encouraging aspect of Mike Polignano's story is that it shows that a smart and inquisitive college student can bypass political correctness and plug into powerful scientific research that supports a race realist perspective. It goes without saying that such research would not be mentioned in classrooms at the vast majority of American universities, except perhaps to call attention to the "sloppy scholarship" and "moral turpitude" of the scientists who produced it. The good news is that well-informed discussions of this body of research as well as quite a few of the original academic papers are readily available online.

As a result, Polignano has extensive discussions of quite a few of the leading figures in this academic movement, including Frank Salter and Arthur Jensen. His encounter with Jensen's research seems to have been pivotal. His column on Jensen in the Emory student newspaper not only caused an uproar on campus, it doubtless led to a deep understanding of the current academic environment. He was subjected to a forum pitting six hostile professors (none psychologists) against an undergrad who was expected to defend Jensen's position.

Imagine his disgust when some professors agreed in private that Jensen might be right but were too cowardly to come out and say so in public. Remember, at least some of these people had tenure and couldn't have been fired from their jobs for expressing agreement with Jensen. But they could be sure that they could forget about being invited to academic cocktail parties or getting any grants from the university for their travel or research. What a commentary on the contemporary academic world:

> I came to realize that an extremely nasty and highly motivated minority of faculty and students held the campus in the grip of fear. The purpose of my public humiliation was clear: It was a warning. Anyone who publicly acknowledged scientific facts or personal experiences about the reality of race could expect the same treatment.
>
> Arthur Jensen is the Galileo of our times. And to its eternal shame, Emory University refused to look into the telescope.

This is exactly the sort of experience that would turn a bright student away from even thinking about wanting to get a teaching or research position in the academic world. Seeing what can happen when one takes seriously the views of someone like Jensen with impeccable academic credentials would certainly be daunting. One could only look forward to hostility, ostracism, and academic unemployment if one went that route. Recent research indicates that graduate students self-select on the basis of their political beliefs: Controlled for IQ, conservatives avoid the academic profession, while people on the left find a welcome home there. Thus the academy becomes ever more one-sidedly leftist.

If there is one thing I wish Mike Polignano had done, it is to write about his personal subjective experience of being the focal point of all this hostility on the Emory campus. Did students walk up to him and angrily denounce him? Did faculty members give him condescending looks, implying that, "as anyone with any brains knows, Jensen is a crackpot"? Was he forced to be a loner, or did he find a group of students on campus who offered social support?

I have had quite a bit of experience with the personal shunning and hostility that views like race realism elicit on college campuses these days. I never did really adjust to it. And in my case, I couldn't rely on anyone on campus who really agreed with me intellectually, although there were a few gestures of friendliness. The result was that encountering faculty members or even some students would lead to a lot of anxiety.

It must have been much worse for Polignano if only because the urge to fit in is much stronger in young people. And while I have tenure, he must have been looking ahead to a life where his views would forever taint his chances of really getting ahead in multicultural America. When a lot of students look back at college, it's a pleasant blur of parties, socializing, and studying — not memories of hostility and ostracism.

People like Mike Polignano are a rare and courageous breed. We need a lot more like him. And we have to find ways to support them financially as they continue their careers as effective writers and activists on behalf of the White majority of America.

Kevin MacDonald, Professor of Psychology at California State University — Long Beach, has pioneered the evolutionary analysis of Jewish religious, intellectual, and political movements as strategies for achieving collective survival, advancement, and influence in his trilogy *A People That Shall Dwell Alone: Judaism as a Group Evolutionary Strategy* (1994), *Separation and Its Discontents: Toward an Evolutionary Theory of Anti-Semitism* (1998), and *The Culture of Critique: An Evolutionary Analysis of Jewish Involvement in Twentieth-Century Intellectual and Political Movements* (1998), as well as *Cultural Insurrections: Essays on Western Civilization, Jewish Influence, and Anti-Semitism* (2007). He is the editor of *The Occidental Quarterly* and *The Occidental Observer* (http://www.theoccidentalobserver.net).

PREFACE

The following essays were written between the spring of 2000 and the winter of 2005. I first began writing as a sophomore at Emory University for the student newspaper, the *Wheel*. My goal from the start was to promote the discussion of White Nationalist themes to whatever extent possible.

The high point of my career as a student journalist came in the fall of my junior year, when I published "Genes May Determine Racial Differences" on October 6, 2000. Of course I knew in the abstract that this would be controversial. But I was not prepared for the storm of outrage that followed, including local and national media coverage.

I held my ground for the rest of the school year, but when my first editorial of my senior year — on the September 11, 2001, terrorist attacks — was rejected without comment, I put down my pen to concentrate on finishing school.

Most of my Emory columns as well as my account of the controversy are found in the "Mike vs. Emory" section below. Other *Wheel* columns are found in the sections on "Sports" and "The Passing Scene."

I began writing again in the fall of 2003 when I was living in Berkeley. I published articles on my website (today it would be called a "blog"), http://www.michaeljpolignano.com/. I was pleased that my pieces were widely reposted on racialist websites, and my own site developed a loyal readership.

The high point of this period was when David Duke invited me to speak at the International European American Unity and Leadership Conference held in New Orleans on Memorial Day weekend, 2004. My talk, entitled "My Awakening Too," is chapter 17 below. I was pleased to learn that it was translated into Swedish and Finnish.

In the spring of 2005, I again set down my pen, partly because I felt I needed to work on my own life, partly out of feelings of alienation from the aberrant personalities, destructive infighting, and stubborn repetition of failed tactics that dominate the White Nationalist movement.

Why publish a collection of five to ten year old opinion pieces, short essays, satires, and reviews? Well, because I believe that they are *good*. Most of them are not dated. The dated ones are still interesting. And a few even proved prophetic.

Would I write these pieces the same way now? Not necessarily. I realize that I was naïve to rely solely on facts and logic when defending myself before a hostile crowd at Emory. My understanding of sex roles and differences is now more nuanced. And, although I accept Kevin MacDonald's analysis of the Jewish Question, I have too often seen White Nationalists who really do "scapegoat" Jews (and other races) to evade taking personal responsibility for their lives. It's one thing to factually document Jewish overrepresentation in movements that are harmful to Whites. It's quite another to blame Jews and other groups for one's personal failings. But perhaps these are topics for my next book.

I wish to thank everyone who helped make these essays and this book possible, including William Pierce, David Duke, Greg Johnson, Kevin MacDonald, Michael O'Meara, Alex Kurtagić, Paul Fromm, and Sam Dickson, to name but a few. I wish we lived in a world in which I could thank you all by name.

This book is dedicated to everyone who ever believed in me, even when I didn't believe in myself. You know who you are.

San Francisco
July 26, 2010

TAKING OUR OWN SIDE

We all have natural partialities: for family over non-kin, friends over strangers, fellow countrymen over foreigners, racial brethren over members of other races. Philosophers from Aristotle to Carl Schmitt have recognized that these partialities are the heart of political life.

But most moralists eye these partialities with suspicion. Moral laws, they claim, apply to everyone, regardless of his relationship to us. Murder is wrong, whether we kill a stranger or a friend. Fairness requires that we judge a stranger by the same standards by which we judge a friend. Moral laws are universal, and universality means that we must be impartial in all our moral judgments and dealings.

For the sake of argument I am willing to grant that moral laws are universal. But I don't think that implies that all of our judgments and dealings must be impartial. Yes, when we have a case before a judge or arbitrator, we want him to be impartial. But do you want your parents to be impartial when deciding whether to send you or the class valedictorian to college? The most impartial judges are strangers to us. But we do not spend all our time with strangers, and kinship, friendship, and other natural bonds of affection do matter.

I grant that it is wrong to murder both strangers and friends, but surely it is worse to murder a friend. We are saddened to hear of the murder of a child. But we are horrified when we learn that the killer was the mother. We react this way, because we think that mothers should be partial to their children, and a crime that violates such natural partialities seems particularly bad. A moral philosophy that holds all murders equally heinous, regardless of these partialities, is simply absurd.

I look at ethics through a biological lens. A proposed moral principle cannot conflict with the survival of the race. Principles incompatible with survival die out along with their adherents. But there is another consideration beyond survival. There are plenty of bad ideas, foolish principles, and destructive lifestyles whose harm falls far short of killing their practitioners, or impeding their reproductive success. The only way to weed these out is to adopt as one's standard not mere racial survival, but racial perfection. And from the point of view of racial survival and perfection, impartiality is folly.

Why is my standard the survival and flourishing of the race, not the individual? I am not an individualist, because individualism ignores the fact that we are all parts and products of biological groups: breeding populations. A race is simply a breeding population that has taken on a distinct identity because it has been geographically isolated, endogamous, and subject to unique environmental conditions for a sufficient length of time.

If the individual, not the group, is the highest value, then under no condition is it right for him to risk or sacrifice his life for the group. This means that the Spartans who fought to the last man at Thermopylae were suckers, but the man who would buy a few more years for himself by condemning the whole race to extinction is a paragon of virtue. The individual who lives only for himself, oblivious to the race that produced him and endowed him with the talents he cultivates or squanders, is a mean little creature, ungrateful to those who came before, improvident of those who will come after, if any. The isolated individual has but one life and one death. But the racially conscious individual realizes that countless forebears live on in him, and he seeks a kind of immortality for himself and them in his own posterity.

But why is the standard the survival of one's own race and not the human race in general? If the races of man lived in harmony and had no conflicts of interest, then of course we should think of the interests of the whole human race. But we are a long way from that point, and haven't gotten any closer during the past 50 years, despite the claims of the mass media.

The reality is: the races are at war with one another. The different human races are distinct subspecies, with distinct temperaments and talents, some of which conflict dramatically. It is an iron biological law that when two distinct subspecies try to occupy the same ecological niche in the same geographical region, there will be group conflict.

This conflict can be terminated in three ways. First, through interbreeding, which homogenizes the two subspecies into a new, distinct breed. Second, through the extermination of one group by other. Third, through the domination of one group by another.

In the case of humans, all three natural options are highly undesirable. The first two involve the destruction of one or more unique races shaped over hundreds of thousands of years of evolution. The last results in a system prone to instability over the long run, as history repeatedly demonstrates.

But since we're rational creatures, humans also have a fourth option: voluntary separation. This last option preserves racial uniqueness and eliminates interracial competition, allowing each race to shape the course of its own future.

No matter what the outcome, to paraphrase Thomas Jefferson about Blacks and Whites in America: "two races, free and equal, cannot share the same country." This biological law dooms all experiments in multiracial egalitarianism. The only practicable multiracial societies have been hierarchical segregated ones like Vedic India, South Africa, and the American South. But in the end, even these proved unworkable. The Indian caste system did not prevent racial admixture, while Apartheid and Southern slavery and segregation are long gone.

Everything we have seen since desegregation indicates the futility of multiracialism. Desegregation has not created the harmonious mixing of the races in freedom and equality. It has simply robbed Whites of the ability to legally protect their living spaces from the incursions of other races. When these incursions occur, there is racial tension and conflict, which terminates only when Whites flee and the neighborhood becomes predominantly Black, or Mexican, or Asian. Those Whites who remain are slowly destroyed by miscegenation or outright murder—both forms of genocide. Racial warfare will end only when groups separate from one another, or when the groups self-destruct due to miscegenation, or one group exterminates the others, or one group dominates and segregates itself from the others.

And make no mistake: America is in a state of racial war. It is no less a race war because, so far, Whites are not fighting back but are in full retreat. They retreat from neighborhood to neighborhood, as one after another reaches the "tipping point" and becomes unlivable for Whites. They retreat from cities to suburbs, from suburbs to exurbs, from states like California to states like Idaho and Montana. But at a certain point, there will be no place left to hide. The whole nation will reach the tipping point, and Whites will finally have to stand and fight for our survival.

I hope that we stand and fight while we are still more than 60% of the population. Our odds of winning would be a lot higher than if we wait until our numbers slip below 50%.

In the midst of a race war, there can be no greater folly than impartiality, than the pious rot that "there is only one race, the human race." Robert Frost once brilliantly described a liberal as a man who will not take his own side in a fight. In a fight to the death, such a policy is suicide.

In every transaction between a partial man and an impartial man, the impartial man is at a disadvantage. When the impartial man has a benefit to confer, the partial man appeals to the other's impartiality and often walks off with the prize. But when the impartial man needs something from the partial man, his appeals to impartiality fall on deaf ears. As social interactions multiply, so do the partial man's advantages at the expense of the impartial man. (The essence of the Jewish strategy of dominance is to practice ruthless partiality while urging their victims to be free of prejudice and partiality.)

Once the impartial man has nothing left to bargain with, once he has been reduced to powerlessness and penury, to what will he appeal to preserve his life and freedom? Impartiality? Universal notions of freedom and justice and rights? These are just pleading words unless one has the power to force others to respect them. But the impartial man has bargained all his power away. Pleading alone will not prevent him from being reduced to a slave or a corpse, and that is what we Whites will become unless we start taking our own side, and quickly.

January 27, 2004

WHITE PRIDE &
WHITE GUILT

Today in the United States and most of the White world, as soon as a White child is old enough to understand language, he is told that he should feel guilt for the crimes of his ancestors. Guilt for finding, conquering, enslaving, and killing off non-Whites around the globe . . . and littering in the process. Guilt, not for his own crimes, but for the crimes of other people of the same race.

But he is also told that he should feel no pride in the amazing achievements of his race. No pride in the pyramids and the Parthenon, no pride in the arch and the dome, no pride in White science and technology and medicine, no pride in the glories of European painting and sculpture and music, no pride in Plato and Shakespeare and Dostoevsky, no pride in the exploration of the globe and the conquest of space. Pride, not in his own achievements, but in the achievements of other people of the same race.

But if it is reasonable to feel White guilt, then it is reasonable to feel White pride.

This is a subversive thought, for if one does a balance sheet comparing reasons for White guilt and White pride, Whites might discover that they have far more to be proud of than guilty of. Then they might decide to resist their dispossession.

Faced with that prospect, the advocates of White dispossession will retreat to the last refuge of ethno-political scoundrels and cowards: individualism. They will piously lecture us that there are no groups, only individuals—that even if the White race has produced more creative individuals than the other races combined, only the individuals, not the race, should be honored—that the only person entitled to feel proud of Edison's achievements was Edison, because he earned it—that nobody has the right to a pride that he has not earned by his own efforts—that people who do feel pride in the achievements of their racial brethren are losers who need to derive self-esteem from the achievements of others because they have no achievements of their own — and so forth.

The individualist argument goes as follows: The only pride we have a right to is pride in our own achievements. Racial pride is pride in the achievements of others. Therefore, we have no right to racial pride.

I will grant that we have not, strictly speaking, "earned" the pride we feel in the achievements of others. But the false premise of the individualist argument is that we have no right to things that we have not earned. We call something of value that we receive from others without earning it a "gift."

But does it make sense to describe the goods passed on by long-dead ancestors and kinsmen as "gifts"?

I think so. It certainly makes no sense to call it an exchange relationship, since there is no way to repay benefactors who are dead or anonymous. Moreover, one of the functions of the Last Will and Testament is to confer gifts after one's death when there can be no possibility of exchange. One can even give gifts to complete strangers and distant future generations.

A creative genius might take money in exchange for his works during his lifetime. But after he is dead, his collected works become a gift to future generations. We certainly cannot return anything to Aristotle or Galileo or Mozart of value equal to what they have given us. They have given us too much and are not around to receive payment.

There is no question that we have a "right" to things that we receive as gifts. If racial pride can be understood as a gift, then we have a right to that feeling.

But when someone gives us a gift, we naturally want to transform it into an exchange. Receiving a gift puts us in someone's debt, which is not a pleasant feeling. But exchange puts us on equal footing, which is more consistent with our sense of dignity and desire for independence. So we satisfy ourselves with the mere pretense of an exchange by repaying our benefactors with thanks.

But how do I thank people who are anonymous or long-dead: my distant forebears and the racial kinsmen who make me proud?

Certainly not by resting on their laurels or by making their achievements a substitute for mine, which is the puerile individualist accusation.

First, we can become worthy recipients of what they have given us by learning to appreciate our history and culture.

Second, since it is impossible to return their patrimony to them, we can at least pass it on to future generations, so that they can continue to live on through their works.

Third, we can thank them by making ourselves worthy of the pride they have given us, by achieving something of greatness ourselves.

Fourth, we can work to preserve and pass on the genetic heritage that has made the cultural heritage possible.

In this time of racial peril, the highest and noblest thing any of us can do is work together to ensure the survival and flourishing of the White race, so it can give birth to new Leonardos and Newtons and Teslas.

But if we have a right to White pride, then do we not also deserve White guilt?

I think "guilt" is the wrong concept, for guilt implies responsibility, and racial guilt implies collective responsibility. A group of people acting together may be responsible for an act. But it is not just to punish an innocent person for a misdeed committed by another member of his race or community.

The proper concept here is "shame," not guilt, for I can feel ashamed of the misdeeds of others without being responsible for those misdeeds.

We have all felt shame at the misbehavior of other people. It is easy to understand when the culprit is a relative or friend and his actions reflect badly on us. But we also feel shame at the misbehavior of complete strangers. Yet I feel this only when their actions are "all too human," meaning that they reflect badly on me simply because, as a human being, I could have made the exact same mistake. They point out our universal human weaknesses and failings.

In the same way, I feel shame for the crimes and follies of other White people, but only if their failings are typical of Whites and thus reflect negatively on me, making me self-conscious of my own racial weaknesses and potential follies.

As for the usual charges against the White race—racism, slavery, colonialism, environmental destruction—I feel no shame for these at all simply as a White man, and no White person should.

Racism—properly defined as a natural preference for and solidarity with one's own kind, not as hatred for others "just because they are different"—is nothing to be ashamed of at all.

Slavery, imperialism, colonialism, genocide, environmental destruction, and the like are all shameful things, and I wish that none of them had happened. But these crimes have been committed by members of all races whenever they have had the means and opportunity. They are all too human, and all human beings should feel ashamed of them.

The only reason these crimes are lodged against the White race in particular is that we were better at them than the others. We defended Europe from the Huns, the Moors, the Mongols, and the Turks and eventually went forth and conquered most of the globe. The other races are probably more ruthless, cunning, and cruel. But we beat them because of our superior inventiveness, superior social organization, and questing, adventurous spirit.

So when Whites are singled out for blame, we are being attacked not for our crimes, but for our virtues—for being winners rather than losers in the brutal struggle between different races for dominion over this planet.

That struggle has not disappeared just because Whites have abandoned their conquests and gone home.

October 9, 2004

THE ETHICS OF
RACIAL PRESERVATION

In *On Genetic Interests*[1] Frank Salter argues that all living things have "genetic interests," namely, each life form has an interest in passing its genes on to the next generation. Salter then expands upon existing theories of kinship and altruism—most notably W. D. Hamilton's theory of inclusive fitness.[2] Hamilton's theory holds that self-sacrificial altruistic behavior towards family and extended family can increase one's own genetic representation in future generations. In other words, under certain circumstances an animal can protect its genetic interests through altruistic behavior even if that behavior hurts the animal's own chances of reproductive success. Salter ventures into new territory by applying this concept to ethnic groups (or "ethnies," the term Salter prefers) whose members share a greater percentage of their genes than randomly chosen people from other ethnic groups. Ethnic kinship thus becomes a natural extension of family kinship.

One does not require extensive genealogical histories to measure kinship between two individuals: kinship can be quantitatively assessed through gene assay data. Salter measures kinship between ethnies using a global genetic assay performed by L. L. Cavalli-Sforza, P. Menozzi, and A. Piazza in the 1980s.[3] It is

---

[1] Frank Kemp Salter, *On Genetic Interests: Family, Ethnicity, and Humanity in an Age of Mass Migration* (New Brunswick, N.J.: Transaction Publishers, 2006).

[2] "Fitness" is the scientific term for the quantitative genetic contribution of one genotype to the next generation relative to other genotypes of the same species. "Individual fitness" refers to such contribution an individual makes by producing offspring. "Inclusive fitness" refers to such contribution an individual makes not just by producing offspring, but also through behavior that affects others possessing the same genotype.

[3] This assay did not measure kinship *per se*, but rather "genetic distance." However, for practical purposes the difference between the two

worth pointing out that the frequently-cited objection that pure races don't exist due to population admixture does not invalidate the concept of ethnic genetic interests (p. 48). As long as average differences in gene frequencies exist between ethnies, distinct ethnic genetic interests exist.

Births and deaths that occur within one's immediate family have a tremendous emotional impact, but the gradual decline of a race due to low birthrates and nonviolent immigration of foreigners does not. Salter gives these losses greater emotional reality by equating them with the loss of specific numbers of children or siblings. Salter explains that these losses are not merely symbolic, nor are they diminished by being spread across an entire ethnic group. The loss applies to every randomly-chosen member of the ethny: "for a native woman it is equivalent to the loss of *her* children and grandchildren, for a native man it is equivalent to the loss of *his* children and grandchildren." The same holds true for every member of the ethny. Accordingly, Salter argues that ethnic genetic interests are much larger than familial genetic interests.

Salter notes that Englishmen and Danes, though the genetic distance between the two populations is not great, are nonetheless distinct. He calculates that if 10,000 Danes were to take the place of 10,000 Englishmen, the loss of genetic interests to the English would be equivalent to losing 167 English children (or siblings). Numerically speaking, the replacement of 10,000 Englishmen with 10,000 Danes is a loss of 10,000 Englishmen. Genetically speaking, it is a loss of only 167, because Danes are genetically similar to the English, so most of the English genes lost are shared by the Danes who replace them. Salter is not claiming that each and every Englishman loses the genetic equivalent of 167 children or siblings, but that the English people as a whole lose this number. Yet each and every Englishman is related to those who are lost. If, however, 10,000 Bantu immigrants replaced 10,000 Englishmen, the genetic equivalent of 10,854 English children or siblings would be lost. How does the loss due to replacement exceed the number of those replaced? Salter explains, "Some ethnies are so different genetically that they amount to negative stores of those distinct genes."

---

is negligible (see pp. 45–46).

Salter shows that interracial immigration is most damaging to ethnic genetic interests: "It requires only 1.1 African immigrants to depress the European genetic interest by the equivalent of one child (or vice versa). But it takes 59.9 Danish immigrants to have the same effect on the English population, or 27 Polish immigrants on Germans, or 42 English immigrants on Irish (and all vice versa)." Regarding America, "Americans of European and African descent have lost, and are losing, the equivalent of millions of children due to post-1965 immigration."

Salter also examines the effects of racial intermarriage on genetic interests. He starts with J. P. Rushton's Genetic Similarity Theory (GST) which states that marriage within one's ethnic group is adaptive because the children that result share more than 50% of their parent's distinctive gene varieties (or "alleles"). This is because parents within the same ethny have many distinctive alleles in common. The theory also proposes that parents of the same ethny may treat their children better than parents in mixed marriages, because the biological similarity of parent and child leads to more intimate bonding. Salter then analyzes how much more related a parent will be to his children if he marries within his ethny rather than outside of it. An Englishman who marries an Englishwoman instead of a Danish woman only gains a 1% greater relatedness to his offspring, but would be 92% more related to his offspring if the rejected potential spouse were a Bantu. That is to say, marrying within his ethny means his children will carry 92% more of his genes than they would if he married a Bantu.

After laying the scientific groundwork for ethnic genetic interests, Salter discusses their ethical and political implications. He writes, "It is parents' duty to care for their children. Do we have a similar duty to nurture our ethnies? . . . When ethnic competition is high, as is the case in competition between members of different races, failure to show ethnic loyalty is the genetic equivalent of betraying a child or a grandchild." He argues that "it would be prudent for a population to defend its most precious collective interest—distinctive genes carried by the ethny—with the most powerful means at its disposal." Yet to date, "no state yet developed has reliably kept its promise as an adaptive ethnic group strategy."

The biggest threat to ethnic genetic interests are "free riders": those whose genetic fitness is increased as a result of behavior that hurts the genetic interests of the ethny. Such free-riding is most destructive to genetic interests when the free riders are genetically very distinct from the ethny they exploit. In multiracial societies such as America, this happens daily as large immigrant Mexican families receive benefits from welfare, schools, hospitals, parks, and national infrastructure to which they did not contribute and which their own ethny is unable to maintain. Free-riding can also occur within an ethny. Corporate elites can (and do) benefit themselves at the expense of their ethny by outsourcing production to Third World countries, through philanthropy that mainly benefits members of a different ethny (e.g. Microsoft's largesse to Blacks), or by swindling investors and low-level employees of their savings through fraudulent accounting practices (Enron). Wealthy executives are far more likely to act in ways detrimental to their own ethny in multicultural societies than in homogeneous societies, because they have less in common with the average citizen.

What sort of state would best counter these threats and preserve an ethny's genetic interests? Salter comes down firmly on the side of ethnic nationalism. To avoid conflict that risks the common genetic interest through aggressive war and elite free riders, he proposes that nationalism be practiced by every ethny in the world. He calls this "universal nationalism." Under such a system, each state would be based on a scientifically-informed ethnic constitution that makes specific reference to protecting the population's genetic interests. States founded on such a constitution would have common interests: minimizing conflict and free riders. Universal nationalism would preserve ethnic diversity by protecting the genetic interests of every ethny, and would also be in the best interest of humanity as a whole.

In the process, Salter derides left-wing political theory, stating, "The intellectual Left has become largely alienated from mankind as an evolved species." He also states that a "concept nation," that is, a nation founded purely for the sake of a particular ideological concept like "freedom," "democracy," or "equality" rather than the defense of a particular people, "is incapable of principled defense against ethnic replacement."

Salter's defense of self-sacrifice for one's people gives a rational foundation for racial activism. A person who foregoes having children of his own to serve the larger interests of his race—one who lives *or dies* for his race—may serve his genetic interests better than someone who leaves a large family but works against the interests of his race as a whole.

Furthermore, many people who already have children are intimidated from open racial activism because they fear for their children. But Salter shows that our genetic interests are broader than our immediate families. Thus, from a genetic standpoint, "It would appear to be more adaptive for an Englishman to risk life or property resisting the immigration of two Bantu immigrants to England than his taking the same risk to rescue one of his own children from drowning."

Salter also gives hope to those who are unable to have children of their own: people who are unlucky in love, people unable to have children because of a physical defect like sterility or a psychological aberration like homosexuality, women who ran out their biological clocks pursuing lifestyles that stymie motherhood, and so forth. Such people can still salvage their genetic interests by devoting themselves to the good of their people.

Salter marshals an impressive array of scientific data to support his analysis, and his writing is clearly aimed at readers with some scientific or academic background. However, his book doesn't require specialized knowledge to be understood, and he provides a concise summary of each chapter at its beginning. The book also covers a vast breadth of subject areas—genetics, evolutionary theory, political theory, and ethics, among others—so those not interested in highly technical scientific arguments will still find the book fascinating.

* * *

On Genetic Interests is an immensely impressive book. But it is not without flaws. To my eyes, the greatest flaw of Salter's argument is its genetic conservatism, which is allied with a kind of genetic relativism. According to Salter, life is all about passing on the genes that have been passed on to us. But what if one's gene pool contains a large number of bad traits, such as high incidences of mental retardation, physical deformities, and mental illness? Should we want to pass on those genes? And what if one's gene pool contains a low incidence of valuable traits like physical beauty, bodily health, intelligence, cooperativeness, fellow-feeling, and good cheer? Wouldn't it be better to increase the frequency of valuable traits, even if that means importing genes from outside our ethny?

For instance, to use one of Salter's examples, what if the English population could be improved by sterilizing retarded, deformed, and insane Englishmen and importing Danish genes (if the Danes happen to have a higher incidence of valuable traits)? From Salter's point of view, this simply could not happen. From the gene's perspective (and thus from the perspective of ethnic genetic interests), "preserving genetic interests" is entirely a matter of preserving current gene frequencies. There are no higher standards—like beauty, intelligence, or mental and physical health—to which we can appeal. There is no point of view we can take on the issue aside from the relative perspective of the English or the Danish gene pool, which would perpetuate themselves to eternity without change.

Salter's genetic conservatism conflicts with the outlook I recommend: genetic progressivism, also known as eugenics. The eugenicist recognizes that there are objective standards by which we can judge the quality of a gene pool and recommends that we create a better future by increasing the frequency of good genes and decreasing the frequency of bad genes in each successive generation. A eugenicist is not against all immigration, just dysgenic immigration.

There is, however, a limit to my commitment to eugenics. I am all for mixing White subgroups if it really can improve the race. (I hope it can, given that, like most Americans, I am a mixture of different European ethnies—in my case, Irish, French, and Italian.) But if we could improve upon the White race by hybridizing it with a non-White race, I would oppose doing so. Such a hybrid might be objectively superior. But it is a successor race, not my race. And I want my race to survive. So there is a point at which I can embrace Salter's genetic relativism, since I cannot weigh the question of my own race's survival "objectively." In the end, I take my own side, simply because it is mine.

By its nature, Salter's theory also rejects as "irrational" the assertion that any particular ethny's genetic interests are more valuable than any others' by virtue of having greater genetic potential. It is a tenet of Salter's "universal nationalism" that every ethny should be able to pursue its own genetic perpetuation free of interference from any other ethny, and no claims of genetic superiority should be able to trump this fundamental right to ethnic self-determination. But I disagree. Salter's viewpoint does not take into account the real-world implications of racial differences.

For instance, if life on Earth were threatened by an approaching asteroid, and the world had five years to save itself, all ethnies would have an overriding common interest in preventing the catastrophe. However, only high-IQ individuals could devise a solution, and ethnies that possessed a greater number of high-IQ individuals would thus be more valuable to human survival than those that did not. They would be more valuable *even to low-IQ ethnies*. (Even Salter grants that this sort of scenario proves that some groups are genetically superior to others in important respects. But he is loath to admit it because he fears that superior groups will start thinking themselves superior and bossing other groups around.)

Colonialism provides another example. The immigration of Blacks into England is a genetic loss to the English. But the colonization of Africa by the English was not a genetic loss to Blacks. The English suppressed tribal strife and introduced Western technology, medicine, and social organization that raised Black productivity, life expectancy, and populations to levels they never could have attained on their own. Thus the genetic interests of Whites are more valuable than the genetic interests of Blacks, *even to Blacks*, because Black genetic interests depend upon White genetic interests, but not vice versa.

I deplore the dysgenic effects of colonialism and imperialism, and I deplore exploitation (whether of other humans, of animals, or of the natural environment) for shortsighted, selfish gain. But the world cannot afford Salter's universal, non-interventionist ethnic nationalism either. Left to their own devices, and aided by White medicine and technology, the other races will continue to breed recklessly and despoil the Earth, destroying themselves — and us — as surely as my hypothetical asteroid. If only Whites had used the world hegemony they enjoyed until the aftermath of the Second World War wisely: not as an occasion for suicidal altruism or base exploitation, but for the good of all life on Earth. And that good has to be understood not merely as the preservation of life, but its ongoing evolution.

Salter's universal nationalism is just another form of "live and let live" liberalism. But only Whites are susceptible to such schemes. Other races will be undeterred in pursuing their ethnic interests at the expense of others. Some, such as the Jews and the Chinese, will even pursue world hegemony. Thus I fear that Salter's universal nationalism, like all forms of unreconstructed liberalism, will only prove a disadvantage to Whites. Moralistic abstractions about fairness and rights will not secure our survival if a ruthless, predatory, and amoral race gains the power to make ultimate decisions about the destiny of life on this planet.

We now have the power to direct the course of our own evolution, and the evolution of all life on Earth. This is an awesome power, for good or evil. All decisions about its use should be made by our conscious minds, and take into account how our genetic interests depend upon the interests of the rest of the ecosystem. They should not be left to our various selfish and self-perpetuating gene pools, regardless of questions of their relative genetic merits. To make conscious decisions about the future of life, however, we need to formulate ethical standards. We need an ethics of racial preservation *and* racial progress. *On Genetic Interests* is an important contribution to the first project and thus is required reading for those who would contribute to the second.

Winter 2005

No Place Like Home

I love to travel and have done a respectable amount in my 23 years. In the Western hemisphere, I have visited 15 states and the Dominican Republic. In Europe, I have visited Italy (four times), France (twice), Germany (twice), Austria, Hungary, the Czech Republic, Slovakia, the old Yugoslavia, and most recently Ireland.

I love to wander around European cities, not just to see the monuments, but to get a feel for life in the present day. I love to try new foods, beers, and wines. I enjoy the challenge of striking up conversations with foreigners and trying out a few native words. I love it when girls speak English with cute foreign accents.

But at a certain point, I am ready to go home. Being in a foreign country gets tiring after a while. There are customs and conventions that I don't understand, so I am always worried about mistakenly giving and taking offense. It is hard for an adult to be put back into the position of a child, surrounded by things he does not understand. It is frustrating to have to grope for words to express the simplest of thoughts. It is tiring to have to think through things that at home are unconscious and automatic. There are not only strange people, but strange toilets, strange doors, strange windows, strange light-switches, strange telephones, strange electrical outlets, strange pillows and sheets. I begin my journey inspired to think of the greatest things in life, but in the end, my attention is stolen by the smallest.

G. K. Chesterton once wrote, "A man's reasons for not wanting his country to be ruled by foreigners are very likely his reasons for not wanting his house to be burned down: because he could not even begin to enumerate all the things he would miss." The same is true of being ruled by foreigners while abroad. You can start making that list of things you miss.

That's why there's no place like home. Foreign places can inspire you. But home, where the petty and routine are pretty much under control and your mind is freed for higher things, is the only place where you can really do productive work, where you can really live.

But for more and more White Americans, there really is no place like home, in a different sense of the phrase.

It recently hit me when I returned from Ireland to the Bay Area. As I stood at the corner of a busy intersection, I realized that literally everyone I saw around me was Oriental, and the signs on the buildings (some of them anyway) were the only things that indicated that I was actually in the United States. And I was not in San Francisco's Chinatown, but in an "ordinary" commercial district in the East Bay. I realized that in some ways, I felt less like a stranger in Ireland than in my own "home." I wondered, "When did White Americans begin to lose their sense of home?"

It began with desegregation. As Blacks began to move into White working-class and middle-class neighborhoods, they brought their criminality, lackadaisical work habits, bad manners, crude tastes, and disruptive, bratty kids with them. For their White neighbors, home started feeling less and less like home. Whites began to leave, and more Blacks moved in.

Soon, the "tipping point" was reached. Neighborhood after neighborhood became unlivable for Whites. Property values crashed, all the Whites—save for a few impoverished and terrified pensioners—fled, and a once thriving White neighborhood became another Black ghetto. And when enough neighborhoods were gone, the whole city or sections of it reached the tipping point. It happened in Detroit, Newark, Camden, the South Bronx, Baltimore, Washington, D.C., the South Side of Chicago, and so forth.

For most working-class and middle-class Americans, a home is one's single biggest investment. The destruction of White property values due to desegregation has never been calculated. It is certainly the biggest expropriation of White wealth since the looting of Germany after World War II. The mass flight of Whites when major American cities fell to predatory Blacks is certainly the greatest act of anti-White ethnic cleansing since the expulsion of fourteen million Germans from their homes after World War II. People have been tried and executed for "crimes against humanity" for far less. When will the architects of these crimes be brought to justice?

The destruction of White Americans' sense of being at home was only exacerbated by the torrent of non-White immigration, legal and illegal, since 1965. A White American born in 1960 felt very much at home, since the US was a 90% White country. The country had many problems, but for the average White American, feeling like he was lost in a foreign country was not one of them. He would actually have to go to a foreign country to feel that way.

Today, the US is around 70% White, and there are vast areas that feel like a foreign country, a whole host of foreign countries: Mexico, the Caribbean, India, China, Vietnam, Cambodia, Africa, etc.

If nothing changes, by the time that same American approaches the end of his life around the middle of this century, the country will be less than 50% White. There will be no place like the home he was born into. He may be the only White person in his neighborhood. His neighbors may speak English as a second or distant third language. He might have thought of moving to a Whiter neighborhood at one time, but the whole country will have long since reached the "tipping point," and there will be no such enclaves left, anywhere, at any price.

Americans, particularly younger ones, need to decide: at the twilight of our lives do we want White America to be a thing of the past, a relic we can only nostalgically recall through reruns of *Leave it to Beaver* and *Father Knows Best*? Or do we want to die knowing that our children and grandchildren have White communities to live in and enjoy?

Social ostracism is a small thing to risk, considering what's at stake. It is time for White men to start speaking up!

January 15, 2004

THE ALL-AMERICAN

It used to be high praise to be described as an "all-American," even more so if you were an all-American from "the heartland."

But what does it mean to be "all-American" these days? This phrase once referred to something specific: a good-looking, athletic, successful, morally upright, predominantly Northern European White man, a man characterized by fair-mindedness, hard work, patriotism, and traditional family values. And even if he wasn't a particularly good Christian, he was certainly no Jew or Buddhist.

The concept of "the heartland" seems to refer to what is most essentially and least dispensably American. We can live without a finger or a leg, but not without a heart. Racially, the heartland consists predominantly of Northern Europeans, since non-Whites and non-Nordics tend to concentrate along the coasts. The heartland represents cultural conservatism, while the coasts contain the strongholds of liberalism and decadence.

The all-American stands in contrast to the hyphenated-American: certainly the Chinese-, Japanese-, African-, Mexican-, and Jewish-American, but also the Irish-, Italian-, German-, Polish-, Swedish-, and any other hyphenated European-American. The all-American is an unhyphenated, unqualified American.

In the past, the concept of the "all-American" represented more than just a national self-image. It represented a norm, an ideal to which young Americans aspired. The all-American signified the kind of man who built this country, the kind of man who made this country work, the kind of man without whom this country cannot survive.

One might argue that a single all-American identity never existed. Irish, German, Italian, and other European immigrants all retained aspects of the cultures of their respective native lands. Regional differences, most notably between the North and the South, have existed since the founding of the country. But out of these different European and regional roots, a common culture and identity have grown.

My father was an immigrant from Italy. He was born in Florence in 1933, spent his childhood under the Mussolini regime, and became attracted to the America he saw in Western movies, an America of self-reliance and limited government. He really was an Italian-American. My mother's parents emigrated from Ireland. They really were Irish-Americans. I honor my ancestors, and I have visited both Ireland and Italy. But in the end, I am neither Italian-American nor Irish-American nor even "Italian-Irish-American." I am just American. All-American.

American culture may be shallow and vulgar compared to European high cultures and even to European peasant cultures. Certainly American cultural chauvinism is preposterous, since our culture could use a lot of cleaning up. But in the end, we have nothing else.

Millions of all-Americans exist today, but the concept has lost its luster, and many no longer identify as such. Whiteness, we are told, is no longer normative. We are told that American institutions and culture will persevere regardless of the racial makeup of the country. As for the mounting evidence to the contrary—the ongoing radical transformation of America by non-Whites—well, that is "diversity," our new "strength" that we are supposed to "celebrate." And if we don't want to celebrate it, we'd better at least get used to it, since by the middle of this century Whites will be a minority in this country. That is, unless we all-Americans do something about it.

Now that anyone of any race can aspire to be an American, many all-Americans have lost their racial identity, and "Americanness" has lost its racial specificity.

Most members of the White majority apparently see nothing unique about themselves, certainly nothing worth celebrating. And even those possessing ethnic European or regional identities increasingly sacrifice them when they conflict with non-White cultures (for instance, the removal of Confederate flags and monuments across the South). Ironically, they do this in the name of multiculturalism, proving that multiculturalism really means one thing: the dispossession of Whites by non-Whites.

Lacking a cultural identity of their own, many young Whites try to adopt the identities of other groups, hence the vogue for all things Negroid, hence the vogue for primitive tattoos and piercings. Can lip plates, scarification, neck rings, and clitoridectomy be far behind?

Today, some pro-White advocates suggest that we all-Americans identify ourselves as "European-Americans." Our ancestors certainly did come from Europe, and "European" is sufficiently generic to comprise the considerable mixing of European stocks in America. The phrase might also be rhetorically useful for advancing the interests of Whites in a multi-cultural context.

But I am still uncomfortable with calling myself a European-American.

First of all, I am hesitant to concede that White identity is on par with every other identity in a multicultural America. Whites, after all, built this country. Non-Whites have made little if any significant contribution, especially if one takes into account the negative effects of their presence. So it makes sense for Whites to see themselves as unhyphenated, unqualified Americans. Furthermore, I don't want to live in a multicultural America. I want to live in a White America, an America where White institutions and culture are normative and any foreigners must either conform to them or get out.

Second, to call myself a European-American implies that I have a homeland other than the United States. But I do not. Europe contains many flags and many peoples, and I am a foreigner to them all. My father wanted me to have dual Italian-US citizenship, and I could apply for dual citizenship in Ireland as well. I may do so in case America collapses. But having grown up and lived nearly all my life in the States, I would be a stranger in both lands.

Mexican-Americans have Mexico, Japanese-Americans have Japan, Chinese-Americans have China, Jewish-Americans have Israel, etc.

But all-Americans, particularly those who have lost contact with their distant European relatives, have no homeland other than America. That is why we must stand and fight to preserve it.

October 29, 2003

POTEMKIN EQUALITY

In 1787 the Russian count Grigori Aleksandrovich Potemkin organized a tour for Catherine the Great of recently annexed territories in the Crimea. Everywhere Catherine went, she saw villages filled with happy, prosperous peasants and concluded that all was well. Potemkin's enemies, however, accused him of fooling the Empress by constructing fake villages, islands of prosperity in a blighted landscape. Since then, the phrase "Potemkin village" has come to mean any false façade erected to hide an unseemly reality.

Affirmative Action is one such "Potemkin" program.

Advocates claim Affirmative Action remedies racial inequality: specifically, it addresses the fact that Blacks, Hispanics, and American Indians are "under-represented" at the top of American society (in higher education, the professions, the upper classes, etc.) and "over-represented" at the bottom of society (in menial and manual jobs, slums, prisons, etc.)

They claim that all ethnic groups would be "represented" at all levels of society proportionate to their percentage of the population, were it not for insidious "discrimination" on the part of Whites. If Blacks comprise 12% of the population, then they should also comprise 12% of the doctors, lawyers, and university professors and no more than 12% of the murderers, rapists, and thieves. Any discrepancy is blamed on White racism. Whites exclude Blacks from colleges *simply because they are Black*, and they put Blacks in prison *simply because they are Black*. And the same goes for Hispanics and American Indians.

While I do not deny that some such discrimination is real, massive evidence suggests it does not explain all, or even most, of the problems of Blacks and other racial groups.

First of all, Congress banned overt discrimination in the sixties. But it soon became clear that Black achievement would not rise on its own. Thus Affirmative Action, i.e., overt discrimination in favor of Blacks, was adopted.

Second, racial discrimination never prevented Jews, Chinese, Japanese, and East Indians from being "over-represented" at the top of American society and "under-represented" at the bottom. (And conversely, no matter how much money and effort are poured into Affirmative Action, Head Start, and other programs, they are not sufficient to prevent Blacks and other racial groups from failing.)

Third, the discrimination theory simply ignores genetic explanations of inequality. A vast array of scientific evidence indicates that, on average, Blacks are genetically less intelligent and more prone to violence than Whites. So even if there were no anti-Black discrimination at all, Blacks would still be "under-represented" in colleges and "over-represented" in prisons.

Egalitarians ignore genetic explanations because genes can't be changed (at least with present technology) but social institutions can—assuming we give the government enough money and power to meddle in our lives. If genetic inequality is recognized as the chief cause of social inequality, then the "equality industry"—and its legions of bureaucrats, mollycoddlers, excuse-makers, brainwashers, and bullies—would be out of business.

Thus egalitarians go to absurd lengths to avoid genetic explanations. They continually add new epicycles to the vast, creaking apparatus of social constructionism. One week we hear that low Black achievement results from low teacher expectations. (Teachers tend to expect high achievement from Asians—and some Asians claim this constitutes a form of oppression.) The next week they blame Black underachievement on the fact that Black parents talk to their children less than White parents. (In California, the state even has an advertising campaign to persuade Blacks to talk to their children.) The week after, they blame "micronutrient" deficiencies. (Your tax dollars are going to rectify that problem as well.)

But let's just accept the egalitarian argument for a minute. Let's forget notions of procedural and legal equality. Let's forget the social costs of not training the best possible people to be doctors and lawyers. Let's just accept that the races are by nature equal. Let's accept that the causes of inequality are entirely social, and that these can be changed. Affirmative Action still does not follow, because *Affirmative Action still does not change any of the alleged causes of inequality.* Even by egalitarian standards, it is a failure.

When a Black with an SAT score of 900 is admitted to college instead of a White with an SAT score of 1,200, we have not created a world free of the White ill-will that allegedly keeps Blacks down. In fact, Affirmative Action creates more White ill-will. Affirmative Action does not create a world in which Black children get all the "micronutrients" and parental care and high expectations and quality education that White children get, so that Blacks and Whites can compete for college admissions on a level playing field. No, all Affirmative Action creates is a world that *looks* like the causes of inequality have been eliminated, a world of Potemkin equality.

Faced with the phoniness of Affirmative Action, egalitarians tell us that, by equalizing social outcomes, we will eventually equalize the factors that cause inequality. By changing the effect, we will change the cause. Nay, by *faking* the effect, we will change the cause. In short, they appeal to magic.

But wouldn't the artificial prosperity of Affirmative Action beneficiaries help their children to close the achievement gap? There is no evidence to support this theory. Even in identical environments, Blacks and Hispanics consistently perform poorer on average than Whites and Asians. The children of wealthy Blacks still perform less well than White children of all social classes.

Affirmative Action can create only the illusion of equality. Thus the higher echelons of our society are becoming a Potemkin village increasingly populated by non-Whites who, regardless of their real merits, have been promoted a rung or two above those merits because of their race. Television and the movies portray a fantasy world filled with dumb blondes and Black doctors, lawyers, judges, inventors, and computer geniuses. But behind the façade hides a vast, squalid reality of false promises, false hopes, and outright falsehoods about race—all premised on the refusal to accept racial inequality as a natural fact.

October 14, 2003

INDIGENOUS PEOPLES DAY

Multiculturalism is not an attempt to "enrich" White cultures by adding sundry non-White cultures. It is an attempt to replace White cultures with non-White cultures—or, more precisely, with fantasies, lies, and sanitized half-truths about non-White cultures designed to make them seem spiritually and morally superior. The purpose is to induce racial guilt in gullible Whites which can be exploited for the purpose of White dispossession.

An elegant proof of this thesis is "Indigenous Peoples Day," which is the multiculturalist replacement for Columbus Day, the holiday honoring the White (re-)discovery of the Americas in 1492. The idea was first proposed in 1977 at a United Nations-sponsored International Conference on Discrimination Against Indigenous Populations in the Americas, which took place in Geneva, Switzerland. It received impetus from the approach of celebrations of the 500th anniversary of Columbus's arrival on Turtle Island on October 12th, 1992. In July of 1990, representatives of 120 American Indian tribes and various human rights, peace, social justice, and environmental organizations met in Quito, Ecuador, and announced the plan to turn Columbus Day 1992 into a forum for denouncing White imperialism, colonialism, genocide, and environmental destruction in the Americas and for celebrating indigenous cultures and their resistance to Whites. (Apparently, "nativism" and anti-immigrant xenophobia are only bad when practiced by White people.)

In the San Francisco Bay area, a "Resistance 500 Task Force" proposed to the Berkeley City Council that Columbus Day be replaced with Indigenous Peoples Day. They did not merely argue that Amerindians deserved a holiday, but that Columbus did not deserve one because he was guilty of genocide. The Berkeley City Council voted unanimously to adopt the proposal, thereby symbolically repudiating all of White history and civilization in the Americas. (In 1990, Berkeley changed Columbus Day to Native American Day. In 1991 the name Indigenous Peoples Day was adopted. After several flip-flops under pressure from both Italian American and Amerindian groups, in

1996 Berkeley adopted the compromise "Indigenous Peoples Day-Columbus Day.") Other California cities followed Berkeley's lead, as did the state of South Dakota.

I have mixed feelings about Indigenous Peoples Day. On the one hand, Columbus did kill, enslave, exploit, and plunder the Indians he discovered out of sheer base greed, and these are behaviors that no civilized society should tolerate.

On the other hand, the frontier between two societies is not civilized. There is no common culture, government, or legal system to adjudicate disputes peacefully. Instead, there are competing systems, i.e., a state of war. The notion that Columbus and the Amerindians could appeal to common moral sentiments of humanity and fair play seems like a sentimental ethnocentric projection when one reads actual accounts of Amerindian cultures.

So it seems foolish and decadent when modern Americans, who have never had to face unsubjugated savages, morally condemn the much tougher men who wrested this continent from them, the men whose blood and sweat purchased the long and enervating peace in which fantasies about noble savages and White guilt could grow unchecked.

What I reject is the use of Indigenous Peoples Day as an occasion to spread lies about the unqualified virtues of the Amerindians and the unqualified depravity of Whites. I am glad that Whites conquered and colonized the Americas. All told, it is a much better place for our presence. I celebrate Columbus Day not because of Columbus himself, but because of the historical transformations he set in motion.

But I grant that the history of White men in the Americas is not just a record of creativity and progress, but also of crimes and follies—written in blood and stained with tears. But the same is true of Red men in the Americas, and of all races of men everywhere in the world. Thus it is transparent anti-White racism to create a holiday where Whites are asked to feel guilt for the crimes of fellow Whites but the other races are exempted from the same moral reflection and instead play the role of accusers.

As first step toward blancing Indigenous Peoples Day propaganda, I recommend Kevin Beary's essay "Life Styles: Native and Imposed."[1] There Beary quotes Bernal Díaz del Castillo's *The Conquest of New Spain*, which chronicles Hernán Cortés' discovery and conquest of the Aztec empire. As Díaz reports, in the town of Cempoala near the Gulf of Mexico:

> Every day they [the Native American priests] sacrificed before our eyes three, four, or five Indians, whose hearts were offered to those idols, and whose blood was plastered on the walls. The feet, arms, and legs of their victims were cut off and eaten, just as we eat beef from the butcher's in our country. I even believe that they sold it in the *tianguez* or markets.

When the Spaniards reached Tenochtitlan, the capital of the Aztec empire and the site of present-day Mexico City, Díaz had occasion to observe the Emperor Montezuma's dinner table:

> . . . more than thirty dishes [were] cooked in their native style . . . I have heard that they used to cook him the flesh of young boys. But as he had such a variety of dishes, made of so many different ingredients, we could not tell whether a dish was of human flesh or anything else . . . I know for certain, however, that after our Captain spoke against the sacrifice of human beings and the eating of their flesh, Montezuma ordered that it should no longer be served to him.

Díaz also describes how the Aztecs performed human sacrifices:

> They strike open the wretched Indian's chest with flint knives and hastily tear out the palpitating heart which, with the blood, they present to the idols in whose name they have performed the sacrifice. Then they cut off the arms, thighs, and head, eating the arms and thighs at their ceremonial banquets. The head they hang up on a beam, and the body of the sacrificed man is not eaten but given to

---

[1] http://library.flawlesslogic.com/lifestyles.htm.

the beasts of prey.

Díaz also describes the widespread practice of slavery in the Aztec empire. In the great market of Tenochtitlan, he saw:

> . . . dealers in gold, silver, and precious stones, feather, cloaks, and embroidered goods, and male and female slaves who are also sold there. They bring as many slaves to be sold in that market as the Portuguese bring Negroes from Guinea. Some are brought there attached to long poles by means of collars round their necks to prevent them from escaping, but others are left loose.

As for the Indians of North America, they were not always the peaceful purveyors of tax-free cigarettes, casino gambling, and earthy wisdom we know today. Beary quotes Francis Parkman's *France and England in North America*, where he describes an attack by the Iroquois on an Algonquin hunting party, in the autumn of 1641, and the Iroquois' treatment of their prisoners:

> They bound the prisoners hand and foot, rekindled the fire, slung the kettles, cut the bodies of the slain to pieces, and boiled and devoured them before the eyes of the wretched survivors. "In a word," says the narrator [that is, the Algonquin woman who escaped to tell the tale], "they ate men with as much appetite and more pleasure than hunters eat a boar or a stag . . ."
>
> The conquerors feasted in the lodge till nearly daybreak . . . then began their march homeward with their prisoners. Among these were three women, of whom the narrator was one, who had each a child of a few weeks or months old. At the first halt, their captors took the infants from them, tied them to wooden spits, placed them to die slowly before a fire, and feasted on them before the eyes of the agonized mothers, whose shrieks, supplications, and frantic efforts to break the cords that bound them were met with mockery and laughter . . .
>
> The Iroquois arrived at their village with their prisoners, whose torture was designed to cause all possible suf-

fering without touching life. It consisted in blows with sticks and cudgels, gashing their limbs with knives, cutting off their fingers with clam-shells, scorching them with firebrands, and other indescribable torments. The women were stripped naked, and forced to dance to the singing of the male prisoners, amid the applause and laughter of the crowd . . .

On the following morning, they were placed on a large scaffold, in sight of the whole population. It was a gala-day. Young and old were gathered from far and near. Some mounted the scaffold, and scorched them with torches and firebrands; while the children, standing beneath the bark platform, applied fire to the feet of the prisoners between the crevices . . . The stoicism of one of the warriors enraged his captors beyond measure . . . they fell upon him with redoubled fury, till their knives and firebrands left in him no semblance of humanity. He was defiant to the last, and when death came to his relief, they tore out his heart and devoured it; then hacked him in pieces, and made their feast of triumph on his mangled limbs.

All the men and all the old women of the party were put to death in a similar manner, though but few displayed the same amazing fortitude. The younger women, of whom there were about thirty, after passing their ordeal of torture, were permitted to live; and, disfigured as they were, were distributed among the several villages, as concubines or slaves to the Iroquois warriors. Of this number were the narrator and her companion, who . . . escaped at night into the forest . . .

Ideally, I would like to get beyond Whites and Amerindians trading atrocity stories about and demanding apologies for the actions of one another's ancestors. But gaining a balanced picture of those atrocities is probably the only way to do this.

In the meantime, if today's Native Americans wish to express shame and guilt for their racial brethren's behavior, what better occasion than Indigenous Peoples Day?

October 11, 2004

THE BROWNING OF AMERICA

May 17th of this year is the 50th anniversary of the United States Supreme Court's ruling in the case of *Brown v. the Board of Education of Topeka*. The decision declared that "separate educational facilities are inherently unequal." This denied the legal basis for segregated classrooms in Kansas and twenty other states. *Brown* marked the beginning of the end of all forms of racial segregation in the United States. And, unless *Brown* and its legacy are swept away, some Chinese historian of the next century will write that *Brown* was the beginning of the end of the United States as a whole.

The establishment is gearing up to celebrate this anniversary with a propaganda blitz. *Brown* will be hailed as a great step forward in race relations. But we will also be repeatedly reminded how far America still falls short of complete racial equality. This should surprise no one, because racial inequality is genetic and cannot be changed by social programs. We will also be reminded that racial harmony remains an elusive ideal—not because Blacks are on average provably less intelligent than Whites and more aggressive, impulsive, and prone to psychopathologies—but because of White racism, ignorance, and criminality. We will be reminded a good deal of James Byrd and other black victims of White crimes. One might even get the impression that the vast majority of interracial crimes are committed by Whites against Blacks, whereas the truth is the exact opposite.

The first purpose of this propaganda blitz is to hide the truth. For if the past 50 years have proved anything, it is that Whites and Blacks cannot mingle in a state of freedom and equality. The rosy predictions of the desegregationists have proved false, and the direst warnings of the segregationists have proved true. The second purpose is to browbeat White Americans into surrendering still more of their freedom and prosperity to the pursuit of the chimera of multiracial egalitarianism.

The establishment is clearly trying to exploit the strange power that some numbers have over the human imagination. People routinely celebrate a 50th anniversary more than a 51st, because although 50 is less than 51, it is a round number, a multiple of 10 and half of 100. Go figure.

But if the number 50 captures the attention of the public, there is no reason why White Nationalists cannot use the "golden anniversary" of *Brown* to point out the truth about race and desegregation. There is no reason why we cannot turn it into a day of mourning, not a day of celebration. There is no reason why it cannot be an occasion for comparing rhetoric to reality and realizing that the segregationists were right. There is no reason why the 50th anniversary of *Brown* cannot be seen, by some White historian of the next century, as the beginning of the end of multiracialism, as the day when America turned from the path of destruction back to the path of greatness.

All we need do is act.

Yes, we have many powerful enemies, but nature and truth are on our side.

February 28, 2004

Scientific American
ON THE REALITY OF RACE

The scientific study of race is at a crossroads. With the mapping of the human genome, scientists know more about race and racial differences than ever before. But as society invests more and more in the lie of racial equality, it becomes harder and harder for scientists to speak these truths. Furthermore, in a desperate attempt to stave off the dire political consequences of racial truth, egalitarian spin-doctors have spread a great deal of disinformation about recent genetic discoveries.

We are told, for instance, that from a genetic point of view the differences between the races are negligible, a matter of just a few genes. Therefore, we are asked to conclude, racial differences are negligible, period. Racial differences, we are told, should have no practical implications at all.

But this is as absurd as arguing that, since from the point a view of subatomic physics, solid objects are mostly empty space, it is a matter of pure prejudice that we prefer to drive on the road and not off a cliff.

The truth is: from small genetic differences, great physical, spiritual, cultural, and political differences grow. If geneticists can't see these differences, maybe they are looking in the wrong place.

We are also told routinely that there is more genetic variation within races than between them. There might be 100 IQ points difference between an extremely smart and an extremely stupid White person. But there is only 30 points difference between Whites and Blacks on the average. Therefore, we are asked to conclude, we should deal only with individuals and ignore the group averages.

The trouble with this argument is that societies do not consist of isolated individuals, for individuals are parts and products of breeding populations. Breeding populations that have become geographically isolated and subjected to different environmental conditions over a long period of time become different races.

And if the average intelligence—or any other important characteristic—of two breeding populations sharing the same geographical area differs dramatically, there is bound to be conflict. The superior group will inevitably resent the retarding effect of the inferior, and the inferior groups will resent the impossible standards imposed by the superior.

But the practical implications of racial truth are hard to deny, and the truth is seeping out, sometimes in unlikely places. A case in point is the cover article of the December 2003 issue of *Scientific American*, which despite its title is usually as politically correct as any news or entertainment magazine. The cover depicts six female faces appearing to belong to different races, along with the caption, "Does Race Exist? Science Has the Answer: Genetic Results May Surprise You." In the table of contents, we read: "Does Race Exist? From a purely genetic standpoint, no. Nevertheless, genetic information about individuals' ancestral origins can sometimes have medical relevance."

This got my attention. If race is medically relevant, then why is it not psychologically relevant, culturally relevant, morally relevant, and politically relevant as well? And if genetic science regards such pressingly relevant distinctions as unreal or miniscule, then isn't there something wrong with genetic science or with our interpretation and application of its findings?

The authors of the article, Michael Bamshad and Steve Olson, argue that "people can be sorted broadly into groups using genetic data." These groups, furthermore, appear to be geographically distinct—at least before the massive population shifts of the modern era. Now this is a huge admission, for the existence of genetically distinct human groups is certainly part of what is meant by "race," and precisely what is denied by those who claim that race is merely a "social construct."

The basis for the claim that "from a purely genetic standpoint" race does not exist is the conflict between genetic classifications and traditional racial categories. Such categories are based not on an analysis of genes (genotype) but on the visible expression of these genes (phenotype). This may well be true, but it does not prove that "race does not exist." It merely proves that there is a conflict between genotypic and phenotypic definitions of race.

For example, the authors note that sub-Saharan Africans and Australian Aborigines look and behave similarly, but genetic markers indicate their ancestors separated long ago. But the conflict between classificatory schemes is more real than apparent, for Australoids and Negroids look alike only to an untrained eye. Anyone who compares members of the two groups will readily see the differences, and with sufficient experience it is virtually impossible to confuse between them.

The authors also note that social definitions of race vary from region to region: "someone classified as 'black' in the US . . . might be considered 'white' in Brazil and 'colored' . . . in South Africa." But this is also an attempt to discredit phenotypic differentiation by referring to only its crudest forms. However, in societies with a great deal of miscegenation, phenotypic classification schemes can be quite complex in order to precisely reflect the complexities of the underlying genotypes:

> The early French colonists in Saint-Domingue identified 128 different racial types, defined quite precisely along a mathematical scale determined by simple calculations of ancestral contributions. They ranged from the "true" mulatto (half white, half black), through the spectrum of *marabou, sacatra, quarterón*, all the way to the *sang-mêlé* (mixed blood: 127 parts white and one part black. . . . The sociologist Micheline Labelle has counted 22 main racial categories and 98 subcategories (for varying hair types, facial structure, color and other distinguishing factors) used among Haiti's middle class in Port-au-Prince in the 1970s. Within each category, the words are often as imaginative as they are descriptive: *café au lait* ("coffee with milk"), *bonbon siro* ("candy syrup"), *ti canel* ("little cinnamon"), *ravet blanch* ("white cockroach"), *soley levan* ("rising Sun"), *banane mûre* ("ripe banana"), *brun pistache* ("peanut brown"), *mulâtre dix-huit carats* ("18-carat mulatto") . . . .[1]

---

[1] Robert Logan, "Hispaniola: A Case History in Multicultural Madness," http://www.barnesreview.org/html/hispaniola.html.

A deeper problem with the authors' emphasis on genotype is that even though different genotypes can give rise to similar phenotypes — nature can use different means to achieve the same end — the forces of evolution didn't give a damn about specific genotypes, they only "cared" about how those genotypes were expressed in an individual. Selection works directly on the phenotype, only indirectly on the genotype. Thus from a practical point of view, phenotype is more important than genotype.

The authors do, however, admit that phenotypic racial categories work well for dividing groups by propensity for certain diseases, such as sickle cell anemia (most common among Africans) and cystic fibrosis (most common among Europeans). The alleles for sickle cell anemia and cystic fibrosis rose in frequency because carriers (i.e., those with a copy from either their father or mother, two copies being needed for the disease) were resistant to parasitic microorganisms found in Africa and Europe, respectively. Another example is that the same polymorphism in the CCR5 gene is shown to retard AIDS progression in Whites but accelerate it in Blacks.

Because of the mounting genetic evidence of the medical relevance of race, the US Food and Drug Administration braved the inevitable controversy and recommended in January of 2003 that researchers collect racial data in clinical trials.

Hence the authors' extremely cautious conclusion: "in cases where membership in a geographically or culturally defined group has been correlated with health-related genetic traits, knowing something about an individual's group membership could be important."

This is another huge admission. For if racial differences are medically relevant, why are they not culturally, socially, and politically relevant as well? For instance, the fact that Negroes produce higher testosterone on average than other races means that Black men are at higher risk for prostate cancer. But high testosterone production also means that Black men are more prone to aggressive behavior. So if doctors should racially profile Black men, why shouldn't policemen?

Compared to Whites, Blacks also have lower IQs and levels of empathy, weaker senses of personal efficacy and responsibility, greater propensities to sociopathy and psychosis, fewer behavioral inhibitions, greater impulsiveness, higher sexual activity and lower parental investment, etc. Surely these racial differences have important practical implications as well.

When you pare away the authors' nervous qualifications and cautious quibbles, "Does Race Exist?" admits that there is a genetic basis for race differences and that these differences have practical importance. This is an encouraging sign in today's climate of ideological Race Denial™. Frankly, it is remarkable that it was published in *Scientific American* at all.

An explanation for its publication might be found in John Rennie and Ricki Rusting's editorial "Racing to Conclusions." They begin by recalling the failure of Proposition 54, the recent California ballot initiative that would have forbidden the government to collect racial data in many areas. Even though Proposition 54 explicitly allowed the collection of racial data for health purposes, many physicians and medical groups claimed the measure would impede efforts to track and treat diseases that afflict various races differently. The editors question these dire predictions, not because the Proposition addressed their concerns, but because they misconstrue the Bamshad/Olson article and falsely assert that its authors firmly oppose the use of racial classification in medicine. One wonders if the article would have seen print if the editors had understood it!

The editors cite the difficulties of racial classification, especially the classification of mixed-race individuals. Then they lament that "race is being used as a surrogate for genetic differences" in research, as if the correlation between the two were insignificant. They point out the FDA's recommendation, and cite J. Craig Venter's remark: "Using self-identified race as a surrogate for testing a person directly for a relevant trait is akin to recording the average weight of a group rather than weighing each individual."

Of course Venter can be expected to oppose racial classification in medicine. By doing so, he's not only being politically correct, he's also taking a position from which he could substantially profit, since his company Celera was the first to sequence the human genome and would likely be the first to mass-market individual genetic sequencing.

The editors omit any mention of the benefits of racial classification in medicine. Those who do not read the main article would incorrectly conclude that race has no use in medicine. Yet another example of how the media spins and distorts the truth. Fortunately, anyone reading the article can see through the spin. However, were a story like this to be covered by the major media, you can be sure that spin is all the viewer would get.

The cover art also reeks of politically correct Race Denial™. The images of six attractive female faces apparently of different races were created by Nancy Burson using a morphing program designed to simulate various racial characteristics. Only the blond, blue-eyed woman is real. The other images were created by altering hers. But one can see that the woman's underlying bone structure, lips, and nose remain unchanged, even though these vary significantly among the races. Only skin color, eye color, and hair color seem to vary. The obvious message of the photos is that race is only skin deep. The world consists merely of White people of different tints. What harm could there be in that?

I'm reminded of a storybook image I saw as a child, where lions snuggle alongside lambs and wolves dance with sheep, where appearances alone differentiate animals that are otherwise, deep down, all the same and thus capable of living in bliss and harmony.

Apparently some adults still subscribe to such wishful thinking.

December 16, 2003

DEFENSIBLE RACISM

There has been a lot of discussion in White Nationalist circles about how to respond to being called a "racist." Does one admit the charge? Deny it? Admit it with qualifications? When our enemies get to define the term to suit their needs, none of the options are very appealing. "Racist" is an indictment, trial, conviction, and sentence—all in one word.

Edgar Steele's *Defensive Racism* deserve praise for offering a new and more palatable definition of racism that may very well gain currency among White Nationalists. According to Steele, "defensive racism" is racism practiced for the love of one's people, in order to assure their safety, survival, and self-determination. Examples of defensive racism include opposing Affirmative Action, practicing self-segregation, and opposing illegal immigration.

Defensive racism is contrasted with "offensive racism," which is practiced due to feelings of hatred or superiority towards other races. Politically-correct Leftists see no difference between "defensive" and "offensive" racism, but thinking Americans do, and aversion to the label of "racist" keeps many quality individuals from joining the White Nationalist movement.

Defensive Racism is a consolidated list of symptoms, a diagnosis, a prognosis, and a prescription for White America. As such, it covers a tremendous amount of ground, and a comprehensive review would be impossible in a single article. I will thus focus on the book's strongest and weakest points.

Steele's concise first-person writing style and his lavish use of wry humor and rhetorical questions give the book a very personal feel. Steele doesn't talk down to or over the head of the reader, but instead engages him in a one-on-one fashion. This style is easy to digest, making the book a quick read, and there is sufficient redundancy to ensure the reader doesn't miss any important points.

That said, the book could have been better organized (the issue of Jewish Supremacism, for instance, is dealt with in Chapters 6, 10, 12, 14, 16, and 17, but not in 7, 8, 9, and only very briefly in 11,

13, and 15). The book also would have been better had it been indexed and annotated (references are included, but lack full biblio-
graphic information and only appear in the body of the text).

The book's primary audience is the uninitiated independent
thinker: the person who has "racist" thoughts from time-to-time
but isn't entirely comfortable with those thoughts or with radical
politics. It's for those who know they've been betrayed by the
Republican Party, but who aren't quite ready for David Duke's
My Awakening.

As someone who was "awakened" back in 1999, I was very
familiar with the content matter of most of the book. I was therefore most interested in Steele's unique personal experiences as a
lawyer, a father, and a racial activist. In Chapter 11, Steele shares
an excellent letter he wrote to a liberal friend who had rebuked
him after he represented the Aryan Nations in a lawsuit brought
by the Southern Poverty Law Center.

In Chapter 12, Steele recounts the experiences of Lonny Rae, a
client of his who faced five years in a state penitentiary under
Idaho's felony "malicious harassment" statute, merely for calling
a Black man a "nigger" after he injured his wife. Incredibly, Rae
was convicted of assault after a jury trial (isn't this the sort of
insanity jury trials are supposed to protect against?), and the DA
never even filed charges against the Black man.

And in Chapter 17, Steele uses his background as a financial
analyst to examine the causes of the next major Depression,
which Steele believes is unavoidable and imminent (I'm inclined
to agree), and to make a case for acquiring gold and silver as an
economic "escape pod."

Even though it is no news to me, racial disparities in crime
statistics never cease to amaze me. According to Jared Taylor's
*Paved With Good Intentions: The Failure of Race Relations in Con-
temporary America*, as quoted by Steele, 60% of all Blacks are
armed with a weapon at all times. Paraphrasing Australian journalist Paul Sheehan, Steele also writes that, "Blacks are raping or
attempting to rape one-half million White American women
each year." If these statistics shock me, I can imagine their effect
on a newcomer to our ideas.

I congratulate Steele for his vigorous and uncompromising

stance on the Jewish question. He relates some of his personal experiences that hardened him on the issue: "trigger events," as he calls them. One was having the law firm he started from scratch nearly stolen from him by a Jew he hired. The Jew acted "so naturally, so matter of course, without a shred of remorse — just like he was entitled to the fruits of my life's hard work." The second was having his kids' lives threatened by a Jewish telephone caller, and having his daughter tell him, between sobs, about the woman who was going to kill her.

The newcomer to the movement will likely immediately view Steele's later statements about the Jews with suspicion, as any intelligent person would question the objectivity of someone whose personal life has been so deeply affected. But Steele does not confound facts with personal animosities. Notwithstanding remarks such as "seems like every time I turn over a rock in America these days, there is a Jew beneath it," Steele does a good job of telling it as it is, though as noted above, footnotes or endnotes would be a nice addition and would help alleviate the reader's potential suspicions.

Steele unflinchingly states that being anti-Zionist isn't enough. The neoconservative Zionist hawks who hurl the charge of "anti-Semitism" at anyone who questions America's unconditional support of Israel are just part of the problem.

The bigger problem is the Jewish community that nurtures the accusers, protects them, and fails to denounce their behavior (usually because they see nothing wrong with it). Just as one is called "racist" for opposing Affirmative Action, one is now called "anti-Semitic" for opposing Israel. (The term "Defensive Anti-Semitism" comes to mind, though it's not used in the book. Jews, however, seem to be the chief practitioners of "offensive racism" as Steele defines it.)

Steele concludes the book with a chapter that depicts one possible scenario for the balkanization of America after an economic and social collapse. His vision includes a period of anarchy and tumultuous racial strife, followed by the formation of several new self-determined nation-states: "New America," "Aztlan," "New Africa," and, amazingly, "New Israel." I found his speculations interesting and occasionally amusing, though they have some flaws. For one, I don't foresee a "New Israel" forming anywhere on the North American continent after America's downfall. Another problem is that Steele fails to address the fate of America's vast military arsenal. I think he is naïve to believe that "New America," "Aztlan," and "New Africa" could remain at peace with one another for any length of time.

He then goes on to propose a form of government for "New America." New America will be a constitutional parliamentary republic with three branches of government. The parliament would be comprised of a Senate, consisting solely of men, two from each state; and a House of Representatives, comprised solely of women, having the same number as the Senate and its membership elected by districts consisting of equal population. The chief executive's powers would be strictly administrative and procedural, with no ability to negotiate with foreign entities or to originate or suggest legislation. The judicial system would be essentially the same as today's, with the exception that juries would be able to rule on matters of law as well as fact. In staffing the system, however, Steele would start over from scratch: all current lawyers and judges would be disbarred, and all existing case law would be rescinded.

I do not have the space for an extended commentary on Steele's proposals, but I do appreciate his thinking ahead and proposing something. He correctly states that we should consider ourselves dual citizens of "New America" and contemporary America. The day will come when we will need to form a new government, and it's good to think a bit about its structure.

Overall, *Defensive Racism* is an excellent introduction for the newcomer to the realities of race, immigration, and Jewish supremacism in America. It is compulsively readable, incisive in its analysis, and deft in its marshalling of factual evidence.

But *Defensive Racism* communicates more than just facts. It also communicates a sense of urgency and the necessity to do something to prepare for America's now-inescapable fate. *Defensive Racism* is so good, I would recommend it to my own mother.

To borrow some of Steele's own words, "*Defensive Racism*—a book whose time has come."

January 24, 2005

EDUCATORS BAFFLED BY
STUBBORN ACHIEVEMENT GAP

The recent release of national SAT testing data brought surprise and disappointment across the nation as the achievement gap between so-called "normal" students and Differently Intelligent (DI) students failed to narrow yet again, in spite of another set of costly federal initiatives directed at closing the gap. The average SAT score for "normal" students is 1,020. The average SAT score for DI students is 610.

The poor scholastic achievement of DI students was once attributed to unalterable congenital or acquired brain defects. DI students were once cruelly stigmatized as "stupid," "subnormal," "imbeciles," "idiots," "slow," and even "mentally retarded." But according to Harvard biologist Stephen Goldfinger:

The idea that Children of Difference suffer from unalterable brain defects was the last bastion of racism. After all, such views were used by the Nazis to justify the mass murder of the Differently Intelligent. Differently Intelligent children are just as good as any other children. The failure to appreciate this is merely a form of intellectual racism. If Differently Intelligent children don't measure up, then it is time to change the yardstick.

In 1980, however, things began to change for the DI when Harvard lawyer Ari Wiesel founded the now somewhat anachronistically named National Association for the Advancement of Retarded People. The NAARP threw itself into intense lobbying on behalf of DI people. They were aided in their consciousness-raising efforts by Hollywood and the television industry, including such Oscar-winning movies as *Forrest Gump*, *Sling Blade*, *I Am Sam*, and, especially, *Shawn* starring Brad Pitt as a young man whose Down's Syndrome enabled him to defeat a plot by evil Scandinavian eugenicists to exterminate everyone not fit to become part of a so-called "smarter" race.

By 1999, the NAARP had secured the passage of a whole series of important bills. There was the Lieberman Bill, which gave
the DI the right to vote; the Wellstone Bill, which gave them the
right to drive; the Feinstein Bill, which gave them the right to
buy guns; the Schumer Bill, which gave them the right to adopt
children; and, most importantly, the Equalization of Opportunity Act, which declared that "retarded" people are just as good as
"normal" people, only "different"; the EOA also outlawed discrimination on the grounds of intelligence and mandated that
governments, employers, and educational institutions treat the
Differently Intelligent the same as anyone else, and give them
special consideration in hiring and promotion, in view of the
discrimination they have suffered in the past.

"Thanks to the Equalization of Opportunity Act, now *every*
little boy and girl can dream of growing up to be President," said
Bill Clinton, as he signed the bill into law, surrounded by beam-
ing Down's Syndrome children and clinging microcephalics.
Giddy with success, the NAARP declared January 1, 2000, the
beginning of the "Millennium of the Differently Intelligent."

Schools around the nation immediately went to work integrating DI and "normal" students. Demeaning "special education" programs were abolished. DI students were placed in the
same classrooms as "normal" students. Federally mandated "affirmative education" programs gave DI students extra help to
overcome the legacy of discrimination. Lavish federal funding
made it possible for each DI child to have a personal tutor.
Meanwhile, so-called "normal" students devoted part of every
school day to tolerance and diversity curricula designed to un-
cover and eliminate the archaic and hurtful intellectual prejudic-
es that are judged the main reason why the Differently Intelligent did not perform the same as all the rest.

In spite of these efforts, the average SAT score for DI students
has remained 610 since tests were first administered. The only
narrowing of the gap comes from the steady decrease of the average scores of "normal" students by about ten points per year.
According to Shelly Zyporen, spokesman for Education Secretary Meeks Ryan:

This trend is merely temporary — the entirely foreseen side-effect of the great strides we have made in integrating Differently Intelligent students into mainstream classrooms. It is a pity that SATs cannot measure the enrichment that so-called "normal" students have received from the intellectual diversity provided by the Differently Intelligent students in their classrooms.

"Naturally, I am disappointed with the latest SAT results," says Shulamith Ratner, the Media Director of the NAARP:

But the Children of Difference have not failed. The System has failed. These children are not retarded. The System is retarded by prejudice and bigotry. The Differently Intelligent are prisoners of society's lower expectations. But five years is not enough time to undo millennia of prejudice and bigotry. Fifty billion dollars is not enough money to ensure that the Differently Intelligent perform the same as everybody else. We need the federal government to commit sufficient funds for at least a generation of concerted effort to change perceptions of the Differently Intelligent. If we change our perceptions, we will change their reality.

Tylenol Washington is a DI student in Oakland. Today is a big day. He is taking his SAT. He is obviously nervous. He is pulling on his left earlobe and rocking violently back in forth in his chair. There are beads of sweat on his forehead. He hums loudly, makes spluttering noises when he is confused, and occasionally blurts out "I'm a man!" Other students seem distracted and shoot him angry glances. But intolerance is forbidden, so none of them complain. After a while, Tylenol is the only student in the testing room. He gets extra time to finish, and he is making the best of it.

Tylenol has just learned that his SAT score is 490. His face beams with pride. But when he sees the circle of grim-faced teachers around him, he slumps forward on his desk, burying his head in his hands, his body wracked by muffled sobs. "He would have received a score of 500 if he simply put his name on it and handed it in blank," says Douglas Strafer of the Educational Testing Service. Tylenol's mother Joretta knows why her son was not informed of this: "President Bush has failed my child. The Republicans, they have slashed our funding and gutted our programs out."

President Bush disputed this through his Press Secretary Dick Zwigoff:

> When we say "no child left behind" we mean it. More than any other President, Mr. Bush deeply deplores intellectualist prejudices against the DI. The Bush administration has spent more than $40 billion on DI educational initiatives. We are proud to announce that spending on DI students is now 100 times higher than spending on so called "gifted and talented" students. The difference between our Republican philosophy and the Democratic approach is that we encourage greater involvement in DI education by the private sector and communities of faith, which will bring even more resources to advancing the Children of Difference.

According to Aaron Liehr, Educational Program Director for the NAARP, testing methodologies are also to blame:

> The Differently Intelligent really are different. So of course their test scores will be different too. But intelligence is a multifaceted phenomenon. There is more to it than just learning facts and solving problems. For instance, the ability to forget is a feature of every healthy mind. Sometimes we need to just let go of past experiences and get over it. But the SATs test only our ability to remember. If they also gave people points for forgetting, I'm betting the achievement gap would be considerably narrowed.

Mr. Liehr made his remarks at the National Holocaust Museum in Washington, D.C., where he inaugurated a memorial to the DI victims of Nazi genocide.

Adam Cohen, the NAARP's Legal Director, held a press conference in Washington D.C. after the SAT scores were announced.

According to Mr. Cohen:

> It is not enough to eliminate all overt and conscious expressions of intellectual prejudice. We must also work to eliminate all unconscious forms of prejudice as well. As long as the DI do not achieve parity, we know that unconscious forms of prejudice must be at work.

Mr. Cohen was somewhat less receptive to another explanation for lack of progress. Mr. Cohen sighed audibly and rolled his eyes as a Differently Intelligent man in the audience laboriously asked why the NAARP itself is entirely staffed by non-DI individuals. "Yes," Mr. Cohen replied, "it is shameful. Look at us. All of us are White, Ivy-League educated lawyers."

The NAARP was founded and staffed by the law firm of Wiesel, Wiener, Liehr, Ratner, and Cohen (Ari Wiesel, JD, Harvard, SAT 1560; Barry Wiener, JD, Yale, SAT 1470; Aaron Liehr, JD, Harvard, SAT 1510; Shulamith Ratner, JD, Harvard, SAT 1520; and Adam Cohen, JD, Yale, SAT 1420). (Mr. Wiener returned to private practice in 1999 after the passage of the Equalization of Opportunity Act and has won multi-billion dollar settlements in class action suits on behalf of DI individuals.)

His eyes growing moist, Mr. Cohen continued:

> But we are committed to filling the next opening for a leadership position with a DI person, and we are proceeding with all due speed to recruit suitable candidates. I am sure that the NAARP will be a much more effective advocacy group once it is entirely staffed by DI individuals. That is the dream of everyone here. I know that I will live to see that day.

Mr. Cohen added that, "The bad news about SAT scores should not overshadow today's good news. After an intensive recruitment drive and a creative retooling of its training program, Delta Airlines has just hired its first Differently Intelligent pilot."

January 30, 2005

"Just Go!"

Last year, before I killed my television, I saw an advertisement again and again that gave me the ultimate solution to the immigration problem, two sharp words to cleave the Gordian knot of casuistic hairsplitting and partisan pseudo-debates.

The ad was for a burger joint called "Jack in the Box." "Jack," the fictional owner, is a tall Whiter-than-White guy. He has a big, round, plastic head, like a snowman head or a Jack-in-the-box head. He talks with a very flat, radio-announcer White-guy voice. He is easy-going, buffoonish, and emasculated. He's the typical corporate White male, who tries to make himself as non-threatening as possible because he desperately hopes he won't get evicted from his box by Jackie or Jamal.

In this particular commercial, Jack is standing in a Mexican-style marketplace. Before him is a typical squat, brown, round-faced, homely Mexican mestizo and her grinning, bobble-headed boy-child. She is selling some sort of searing Aztec emetic made from smoked jalapeño peppers called "chipotlé." But Jack, the hopeless ultra-Gringo, cannot pronounce it correctly.

An aside: why do Peter Jennings and other media lefties take such pride in pronouncing Latin-American names and places with Spanish accents? Don't they realize how ridiculous they sound? Whenever Jennings would say "NEEEcaraGUA," I expected to hear a flourish of flamenco guitar and some castanets. They never say "Paree" or "Köln" or "München." They don't even say "MaDREED," which is proof positive that they are merely pandering to America's brown invaders. But back to Jack.

Jack can't pronounce "chipotlé" properly. "Chipootle" he volunteers meekly, eager for approval, his smiley face replaced by a scribbled, loopy line. To which the woman replies in the international language of Loud and Slow, her words clearly enunciated, her voice clearly annoyed, "CHIPOTLÉ." After a couple of more unsuccessful tries, the patronizing squaw sighs in frustration and says in perfect English, "Just go!"

I was thunderstruck! It was a revelation: I saw the error of our

White ways. We are too polite, too concerned to accommodate and demonstrate goodwill to non-White invaders. These invaders, moreover, do not share or reciprocate our sensibilities, but they are all too willing to exploit them. For instance, they are none too concerned to pronounce English words correctly, or even learn the language at all, but they will correct us haughtily for mangling their dialect.

That's because they probably think it condescending and contemptible for us to try to speak to them in their own language. And it is: We are the hosts. They are the parasites. We created this country. They are invaders. They are trying to take advantage of a system they could never have created and can only destroy—and we will have to work even harder to pick up the pieces and clean up the mess, so they can exploit us once more.

In stooping to their level, we are patronizing them. It is they who should be sucking up to us, trying to please us, worrying about our opinion of them, not the reverse. We are going out of our way to cater to them; we are making them feel comfortable in their ignorance, stupidity, and sloth. Instead we should be rounding them up by the millions and sending them home. But the invaders don't seem to be the least bit worried about that.

White people need to stop making the invaders comfortable and start making them worry. And now, thanks to TV, I know what to say: "Just go!"

"MEEEster, wheeech way is . . ."

"That's 'mister.'"

"MEEEster . . ."

"No, it's 'mister.'"

"MEEEster . . ."

At this point, you must sigh audibly and then firmly say, "Just go!"

It's so simple even George W. Bush could do it—if he really, really concentrates and tries hard.

"Just go!" simplifies the immigration debate immensely. It is the intellectual equivalent of keeping your eye on the ball. No matter what the alien says, always keep firmly in mind that in the end, he must "just go."

For instance, a friend in the Bay Area recently saw a T-shirt saying "Deportation Breaks up Families." He is a big-hearted and earnest guy, and he found the point challenging. When he asked my opinion, I just focused my mind on the bottom line: "Just go!" The answer became clear: "Then send the whole damn family back!"

After all, immigration breaks up families too. Instead of using family unity as an excuse for more immigration, let's use it as an excuse for more thorough deportations. "What, your grand-mother is still in MaNEEELA? Well, we're sending you all back to keep her company. Just go!"

The fact that a two-edged sword like family unity has been used for decades as a tool for chain immigration rather than mass deportation demonstrates three things: the intellectual flimsiness of the pro-immigration advocates, the intellectual flabbiness of mainstream conservative critics of immigration like Pat Buchanan, and why it was necessary for the establishment to marginalize radical and principled opponents of non-White im-migration like Sam Francis. Non-White immigration cannot stand up to even cursory criticism, once White men focus their minds on the bottom line: "Just go!"

It is not the last word in the immigration debate, but it should be.

                                        March 31, 2004

A Revolutionary Act

I believe that the fall of our multi-racial, multi-cultural regime will closely resemble the fall of Communism in Eastern Europe and the Soviet Union. It will occur just as suddenly and unexpectedly, and will spring from equally humble acts of courage, responsibility, and good will.

At the beginning of 1989, Communism seemed invincible. It was guarded by the greatest apparatus of coercion and terror the world has ever seen, an apparatus that had murdered tens of millions of people and subjugated countless others. Communism also controlled the second greatest propaganda machine ever created—second only to the "free" media of the West.

None of the experts predicted the imminent fall of Communism. And they surely would have scornfully dismissed such a prediction. Yet fall it did.

Communism fell because it was founded on a lie. Although few believed this lie, the regime held on to power by intimidating most people into keeping their doubts to themselves. Each individual thought that he was alone because he was afraid to express his doubts to others and others were afraid to express theirs to him. The system fell when enough people took the risk of speaking against its lie, enough that the regime hesitated to crush them. In that moment of hesitation, a space of free communication was opened, millions discovered that they were not alone, the repression and isolation collapsed, and freedom was born.

America's regime is based on the same fundamental lie as Communism: the lie of human equality. Only rather than expressing this lie through a command economy and the suppression of individual entrepreneurship our regime expresses this lie through policies premised on two phony ideas. First, the idea that racial groups cannot differ on average in innate quality. Second, the idea that any observed differences in societal outcomes between racial groups result solely from past or present oppression of one group by another.

We White Nationalists are not alone in believing that racial equality is a lie and that a multi-racial society based on it won't work. I am convinced that many outside the White Nationalist community believe it too. The present regime has victimized virtually every White, and millions are aware of this fact. But most have been intimidated into silence and think that they are alone. Or worse, they have been convinced by the media that only unsavory or outright dangerous people share their beliefs: "rednecks," skinheads, and bizarre Hitler cultists who live in "compounds."

Ideas are not judged by logic alone. They are also judged by the individuals who espouse them. The most radical ideas will seem plausible to some simply if they are expressed in a measured way by a socially "respectable" spokesman—i.e., someone who is polite, well-spoken, educated, and of manifestly good character.

Desegregation triumphed not only because segregationist ideas were dismissed as false, but also because the segregationists themselves were portrayed as ignorant, inbred, and stupid. Intelligent and successful defenders of segregation never received any media attention. And to this day, people associate racism with stupidity and ignorance, even though it is the only scientifically-informed and morally-enlightened position to take.

One cannot readily counter these stereotypes through the anonymity and impersonality of the internet, making face-to-face persuasion necessary.

One of the most important subversive, revolutionary acts a White Nationalist can do is creating a space for free, in-person discussion of racial inequality and the threat posed to White survival by multi-racialism, multi-culturalism, and unlimited immigration.

Begin with your friends and family. Some of them might already agree with you. How will you know, unless you are willing to take the risk of talking to them? I am amazed at how many White Nationalists refuse to talk about their beliefs to their families, even to their children!

Run through a list of people you know. Ask yourself which ones live with their eyes open, which ones have direct experience with non-Whites, which ones have the courage to buck social trends. Then all you need do is take them aside, one by one, in a comfortable, safe, and private place and speak frankly.

If one responds defensively, according to script, don't give up too early or too easily. Try to bring the conversation down to the level of personal experiences. Most people are not interested in abstract theories unless they can be shown to explain their own concrete experiences.

More often than not, I suspect you will be surprised at how receptive your friends and family really are. We have the truth on our side, and plenty of thinking individuals see through the lie but have no one with whom to share their feelings.

Even if a friend or relative rejects everything you say about race, he will still have learned important lessons. First, he will have learned that intelligent, articulate, respectable people are racists, so it is all right if he is one too. Second, he will have learned that some are unafraid to dissent from racial orthodoxy. Third, he will have learned that he can go to you if he ever wishes to discuss matters further. Just make sure to leave the door open to future conversations.

Eventually, after a series of individual conversations, you might want to get a few individuals together for more in-depth discussions. And once you feel comfortable talking to friends, develop your skills in talking to strangers.

Those who do not feel quite ready to speak out should at least become good listeners. Being receptive to the awakening racial consciousness of others is enormously valuable. Simply cultivate a reputation for being "politically incorrect" and open to heretical ideas, and you will soon hear radical ideas coming from the most unexpected sources.

Now that the holidays are upon us, a lot of us get to see friends and relatives we don't ordinarily see. Don't spend this holiday season gorged on turkey and vegetating in front of a football game. The holidays are a time when we can reflect on who we are. Traditional gatherings remind us that we have a collective past and a collective future. They are ideal for having a serious conversation about our future and what threatens it.

You know the truth, so pass it on, and remember George Orwell's oft-quoted words: "During times of universal deceit, telling the truth becomes a revolutionary act."

December 4, 2003

WHY I AM NOT
A CONSERVATIVE

Earlier this week I was walking across the U.C. Berkeley campus with a friend who considers herself conservative. We agree on most issues, although we differ on our views about religion and related social questions. I met her for lunch at Sproul Plaza, Berkeley's traditional hotspot for soapbox oratory, where a hardcore Christian speaker had stationed himself. The speaker had a large sign proclaiming that we either had to "follow Jesus or go to hell." My friend rejoiced while he inveighed against the degeneracy and social decay that dominate Berkeley. I admired the man for bucking the trend but largely disagreed with his message.

Until about a year into college, I considered myself a Catholic and a Republican. Although I didn't agree with the Church's dogma in its entirety, I nonetheless viewed Christianity as a force for good in an increasingly corrupt, debased, and rootless world. I attended a Jesuit boys' high school, and was very impressed not only with the education I received but also with the school's attempt to develop a student's character as well as his intellect. The Jesuits are the most liberal order of Catholics, and even their religion classes were far from dogmatic, encouraging questioning and critical thought rather than blind acceptance.

I also saw the Republican Party as the defender of traditional American values. I remember watching Pat Buchanan's closing speech for the 1992 Republican National Convention on TV with my father. Buchanan looked at the Presidential election as a key battle in America's "cultural war," the struggle between those wishing to preserve core American values and those seeking to change them. He told the story of two soldiers who helped to take Los Angeles back from the Black mob that had taken over after the Rodney King verdict was announced. I was moved by his words, happy to know the Republicans stood for patriotism, morality, and law and order in a time of selfishness, decadence, and racial strife.

I supported the Republicans for the same reason I supported the Catholic Church: not because of what they stood for, but because of what they seemed to stand against. You see, I was a conservative. I worried primarily about social and cultural decadence and decline, and I saw the Church and the Republicans as bulwarks against them.

Only when I got to college did I abandon the Republicans entirely. I already knew that multiculturalism debases all cultures subjected to it, but I was unaware of how much evidence supported the theory that cultural differences between races weren't purely environmental in origin. At the same time I was making these discoveries, the Republicans seemed to be bending over backwards for the votes of minorities who would almost certainly vote for the Democrats anyway.

I ceased being a Catholic and a Republican as soon as I ceased being a conservative.

Today I am a conservative in only one sense: I wish to conserve the White race. But the conservative movement is no ally in this cause. Conservatives don't exactly support Whites becoming a minority, but they aren't willing to oppose it vigorously for fear of being called "racists." Instead, conservatives waste their time and energy fighting over far less important matters: school prayer, abortion, homosexuality, Confederate monuments, classical education, Constitutional law, school vouchers, etc.

Conservatives fail to recognize that everything in Western civilization worth conserving springs from the creative potential of the White gene pool. If that gene pool is destroyed, all of these things will be lost. Conversely, if the White gene pool is preserved, then even if present-day civilization is completely destroyed, we could eventually create a new and even better civilization. It seems laughable to be concerned about whether the Western classics are taught in our schools, but to be indifferent as to whether any Whites are around to appreciate them, much less create new Western classics.

Let's look at a few issues where conservatism is nothing but a liability to White nationalists.

Abortion. Almost all conservatives reflexively oppose

abortion. But from a racial perspective, abortion in the present circumstances is a good thing, simply because non-Whites abort far more frequently than Whites, thereby postponing the date that Whites become a minority. Yet conservatives routinely make a point of mourning the fact that (miscarriages excluded) over *one third* of Black fetuses are aborted, according to data from the Centers for Disease Control.

Homosexuality. Recently the Episcopal Church in the United States ordained an openly gay Bishop. This decision was most vociferously condemned by African Episcopal leaders, who may sever ties with the American church. Most conservatives have sided with the Africans, but from a racialist point of view, this split is a very good thing. The Episcopal Church in the US currently sends tens of millions of dollars to African churches and helps Africans to emigrate to the US. If the Church severs these ties, so much the better for Whites.

Patriotism. Most conservatives are patriotic. White Americans sick of the selfishness and decadence around them desperately want to believe in something higher than themselves. White people who are increasingly victimized by the present regime—which bows to Jews and coddles non-Whites, which taxes them to support non-Whites at home and ships their jobs to non-Whites overseas—still desire to think of America as their own. They cling to the very regime that is abusing and destroying them. This is why conservative Americans were so easily mobilized to fight in Afghanistan and Iraq after 9/11.

The very Jews who preside over the ongoing poisoning of our cultural atmosphere, who sneer at all forms of patriotism except Zionism, who have subverted American foreign policy and placed Jewish interests above American interests, needed money and cannon fodder to kill their enemies in the Middle East. So, with a cynical spin of the propaganda dial, our "liberal" media became "conservative" overnight and patriotic Americans were stampeded into war. (And practically overnight, another Jew produced a book deploring America's "conservative" media.)[1]

Now that the "glorious" and all-too-easy initial slaughter of Afghans and Iraqis is over and our occupation forces are sitting ducks for reprisals by the relatives of the dead, it is White Americans who are over-represented on the front lines and thus among the casualties. But Saddam's ultimate revenge might be the ruinous expense of this war, a cost borne disproportionately by Whites as well.

Unlike the anti-war left, I am not opposed to patriotism as such. In fact, I think it is noble. What I am opposed to is the obscene spectacle of White Americans being manipulated by their patriotism to waste their blood and treasure in a war instigated by and fought for the benefit of Jews. Patriotism just blinds us to the anti-White nature of the present regime. It is time we transfer our patriotism to the one entity that deserves it: our race.

Christianity. Most conservatives are Christians, and even those who are not often cling to Christianity because they see it as an integral part of Western civilization. But it is not. Christianity is profoundly foreign to the European heart and mind. It is a product of Jews and the degenerate, racially mongrelized toiling classes of the Roman Empire. It was imposed by force upon Europe by ambitious kings who desired the meeker, more sheep-like populaces that the Christian virtues encourage. Christianity was made palatable to Europe only by blending it with indigenous pagan customs.

Christianity has always been dysgenic: encouraging the smartest to become celibate, the noblest to spill their blood in senseless wars, and the least valuable to be fruitful and multiply for they shall inherit the earth. Today, Christian churches aid the explosive growth of non-White popula-

---

[1] Eric Alterman, *What Liberal Media? The Truth about Bias in the News* (New York: Basic Books, 2003).

tions, enable non-Whites to flood into White lands, and morally disarm Whites from resisting by telling them that there is no virtue in racial self-defense, only in racial suicide. But if we are meek, we shall inherit nothing: we shall cease to exist as a race.

Conservatism is nothing but excess baggage for White nationalists. In a time when present trends threaten in the long run the very existence of the White race, there is only one moral imperative and one political issue: our survival. In any political situation, there is only one question that matters: "Is it good for White people?"

November 9, 2003

A PARTY OF OUR OWN, PART I

The majority of Americans are White.

The majority of White Americans do not support more immigration, especially non-White immigration, and they want our present immigration laws enforced. But still America is flooded by massive legal and illegal immigration.

The majority of White Americans do not believe in "Affirmative Action" and other programs that give education and employment to non-Whites at the expense of Whites. But such programs continue.

Why? Because neither the Republicans nor the Democrats are interested in protecting and advancing the interests of White Americans. Both parties instead cater to the ethnic special interests of Jews and non-Whites, forcing the White majority to foot the bill.

Democrats see a clear political advantage in such policies, since an overwhelming percentage of Jews and non-Whites vote for Democrats.

The Republicans, however, sacrifice White interests as a matter of sacred principle. The Republicans enjoy power only because of White voters, especially White male voters. But they bend over forwards and backwards to appeal to Jews and non-Whites who hardly ever vote for them anyway.

Not only do the major parties take the White majority for granted, they label Whites who object to their anti-White agenda and wish to protect White ethnic interests as "racists." Yet when Jews and non-Whites pursue their ethnic interests openly, we're told such pursuits are a blessing of "diversity," America's greatest strength (or so they say).

I am sure a substantial number of White people in the Republican Party are racially conscious to some extent. They occasionally even propose policies to advance White interests. But they feel they must cloak all such proposals in universalistic rhetoric.

Republicans oppose Affirmative Action not because it harms

the interests of the White people who vote for them, but because of a rosy vision of an individualistic, "color-blind" meritocracy. And if they mention ethnic interests at all, it is only to lament how Affirmative Action leads people to discount the achievements of genuinely talented non-Whites.

Free-marketers defend freedom of association, but not because it would allow Whites to exclude non-Whites from their living and working spaces. Instead, they talk about the universal rights of all featherless bipeds. And when they mention ethnic interests at all, they argue that the market would work against racism, not for it.

It must be hard to fight for something that you are afraid to name, because all this clever, under-the-radar advocacy of White interests never really makes much headway. It does, however, keep racially conscious Whites voting for a party that continually betrays them. Maybe that's all it is ever meant to do.

It is absurd that in a democratic republic no political party will openly fight for the interests of the majority.

It is amazing that no ambitious political leader has stepped forward to represent the majority.

That's why it's time to form a White People's Party.

The sort of party I envision would have a single goal: to protect and advance the interests of Whites in today's multicultural, anti-White America.

The White People's Party would pursue White interests within the present multiparty political system and the framework of the US Constitution (including the constitutional procedures for amending it).

The White People's Party would represent the interests and pursue the support of all White people. It would set aside issues that divide Whites while seeking to unite us around the most important issue of all: our survival. Unless our survival as a race is assured, none of the issues that divide us matter anyway.

By "White people," we mean people of European descent. If there are any questions about particular individuals we could, as a rule of thumb, ask them to demonstrate their European ancestry for at least four generations back.

The White People's Party would not accept the membership

or support of Jews and non-Whites. We would not work for their interests, and we could not expect them to sincerely work for ours.

Here are some concrete suggested platform points for a White People's Party:

1. Abolish Affirmative Action and Racial Quotas: The WPP would end all racial quotas and preferences that give non-Whites educational and economic advantages at the expense of Whites.

2. Protect Freedom of Association: The WPP would stand for absolute freedom of association and disassociation. It would therefore abolish all so-called "anti-discrimination" laws that force people to associate with people with whom they prefer not to associate and prevent them from forming exclusive voluntary associations. If Whites wish to live in all-White neighborhoods, patronize all-White businesses, and attend all-White churches and schools, they may do so.

3. Preserve the White Majority: America grew to greatness because of an overwhelmingly White majority. But if present demographic trends continue, Whites will be a minority in America in less than 50 years. The WPP would, therefore, halt and then reverse the erosion of the White majority.

4. End Non-White Immigration: The WPP would end non-White immigration completely, deport all illegal non-White immigrants, and then repatriate all non-White immigrants who have arrived since 1965, as well as their descendants. If it was possible to bring them here, it will be possible to send them back.

5. Pro-White Family Policies: The WPP would promote policies that encourage Whites to have larger families and make it possible to spend more time with their children. Conversely, the WPP would make sterilization, birth control, and abortion available to non-Whites free of charge.

6. Put American Economic Interests First: The WPP would put the economic interests of American citizens before the interests of international capital and multinational corporations. To this end, the WPP would greatly reduce income and capital gains taxes and replace the lost revenue with tariffs on imported manufactured goods. This would spur economic activity while protecting American workers.

7. An America-First Foreign Policy: The WPP would adopt a foreign policy that puts American interests first. Never again would American soldiers die for the interests of foreign peoples and multinational corporations. Currently the United States has deployed troops in more than 150 countries around the world. We have more troops guarding the border between North and South Korea than we do guarding our own border with Mexico. The WPP would bring these troops home. The US would no longer play the role of the world's policeman. In particular, the US would no longer give aid to Israel, the greatest threat to world peace, but will instead adopt a neutral stance in the Middle East. To achieve a balance of military power, the US would sell arms to Israel's neighbors.

8. End Foreign Influences: To prevent foreign subversion of the American government, no American would be permitted to hold dual citizenship status. White Americans who hold dual citizenship status would need to renounce the citizenship of their choice. Furthermore, since Jews are the most destructive agents of foreign influence in America today, all Jews would be stripped of American citizenship and encouraged to move to Israel. Finally, no foreign national would be allowed to work in or own industries that vitally affect the national interest, including politics, law, the military, medicine, the media, teaching, banking, investment, etc.

9. Crack Down on Crime: Since non-Whites account for a disproportionate amount of violent crime and Jews account for a disproportionate amount of white-collar and vice-related crime, the WPP would mandate racial profiling as a tool for fighting crime. The WPP would also sterilize felons convicted of violent crimes.

10. Reform the Welfare State: A decent society provides a safety net for the unemployed, the disabled, and the elderly. Since productive people fund such programs, however, they should be reformed so as not to overly burden the productive. The WPP would also abolish all programs designed simply to redistribute income for the purpose of forced equality. The WPP would, furthermore, disqualify people from voting while on public assistance.

11. Encourage Self-Employment: Self-employed people are freer to speak their minds and be active citizens. Therefore, the WPP would adopt policies to increase the number of self-employed people.

12. Protect Freedom of Speech: The WPP would protect freedom of speech and thought by abolishing all so-called "hate crimes" laws, which seek to criminalize thought. The WPP would also break up mass media conglomerates that control and distort the free flow of information.

13. Reform Education: The WPP would end all forced school integration, which retards the education of White children by putting less-intelligent non-Whites in their classes. The WPP would also end all race-based college admissions policies and adopt a strict meritocracy. Furthermore, the WPP would require that all colleges and universities that receive federal funds and have endowments sufficient to cover the cost of education to abolish tuition and admit students purely on the basis of merit. The best universities in the country should educate the brightest, not the richest and best-connected. Finally, the

WPP would, out of considerations of national security and competitiveness, severely curtail the policy of educating foreign nationals in American universities.

14. Insure Voter and Juror Quality: Stupid and ignorant voters lower the quality of public decision-making. Stupid and ignorant jurors cause miscarriages of justice. The WPP would, therefore, require that all prospective voters and jurors pass tests measuring their intelligence and education.

15. Gun Control: Whites are far more likely than non-Whites — particularly Blacks, Amerindians, and Mestizos — to use guns responsibly. Therefore, the WPP would ensure the freedom of Whites to own guns while restricting the freedom of non-Whites.

These are just suggestions, but they give some idea of the platform a White People's Party would have. This platform is not consistently conservative, liberal, or libertarian. But it is consistently pro-White. The White People's Party would be most accurately characterized as "populist," but it is not for "the people" in general, only White people.

A political party is not something to be proposed lightly. There are many more issues to be discussed: How would such a party be organized? What would its electoral strategy be? What about "ideology"? How would a White People's Party relate to other pro-White organizations? How would it handle political issues not directly relevant to White survival?

November 16, 2003

A PARTY OF OUR OWN,
PART II

In the previous chapter, I proposed the formation of a White People's Party to protect and advance the interests of Whites within the present political system. I also proposed some planks for a White People's Party platform.

I received many letters responding to my proposal. All were friendly, most were supportive, and a few were critical. I wish to respond to some of those criticisms here.

THE IDEOLOGY QUESTION

As I see it, a White People's Party should not be for liberalism, conservatism, socialism, capitalism, nationalism, libertarianism, environmentalism, or any other "ism." It should only be for the interests of White people, and none of these ideologies are *consistently* pro-White.

Some think that a pro-White political party requires more than a platform of concrete proposals. They think that it requires its own ideology, a statement of general philosophical principles, an abstract worldview.

I find this idea quite seductive, because I am very interested in political ideologies. But in the end, I think it would be a mistake to base a White People's Party on an abstract ideology. Instead, a White People's Party should merely propose concrete measures that serve White interests and show how all the other parties betray them.

There are several reasons for this.

First, none of the major parties has an official ideology, and a political party that tries to sell a whole ideology would be regarded with suspicion by most Americans, who would see it as somehow "foreign."

Second, it's far easier to get people to accept the simple idea of protecting White interests than to accept an entire raft of ideological tenets.

Third, more people can agree on a concrete platform than on

an abstract worldview. Just consider the different ideologies represented in the pro-White movement today. What little co-operation there is would disappear if all White Nationalists first had to be neo-Confederates, or Odinists, or National Socialists.

Fourth, the opponents of a White People's Party would natu-rally prefer to steer political debate away from specific policies that affect the interests of White people. They would prefer to "refute" these policies by linking them in the public mind to un-savory personalities and ideas, and there is no reason to make their job easier.

Fifth, a White People's Party whose only fixed principle is "to defend White interests in today's America" could serve as a "Big Tent" for all manner of pro-White individuals and organizations. Currently, the pro-White movement consists of numerous groups and organizations espousing sharply contrasting ideo-logical tenets. A White People's Party that does not address dee-per ideological or philosophical questions, but instead offers a concrete pro-White platform, would not seek to challenge or re-place currently existing pro-White organizations, but it could provide a common ground for cooperative effort.

THE UTOPIANISM QUESTION

Some of my critics seem to be utopians. Now, I find utopias seductive, particularly those of my critics. Utopias are seductive precisely because they are so different from present day reality. But they are problematic for the very same reason: It is hard to get there from here.

One of my critics, for instance, was dismayed that my sug-gested platform contained nothing about sending all non-Whites somewhere else. Another said that a political party was undesir-able, because the whole democratic system is undesirable and should be replaced with some sort of aristocracy.

But in today's world, these proposals are political non-starters, and if you are not willing to start with anything less, then there is no point to starting political activity at all. The only thing one can do is daydream about scenarios of economic col-lapse, race war, and violent revolution, for perhaps then such proposals would have a chance.

But I would like to do something in the meantime.

I think it is helpful to have a utopian vision of an ideal society. It can serve as a lodestar for navigating the stormy seas of politics. But when one decides not to sail *by* one's lodestar, but instead to sail *to* it, then it becomes worse than useless; it becomes a danger and a distraction.

Human beings have very little power to control events. Thus I do not view political activity as utopia-building. Instead, its aim is to take steps, in the here and now, to stop the social trends that, in time, will destroy the White race and to set in motion new trends that will preserve it.

There is no way of predicting what form society will take after such policies are allowed to work for a couple of generations. But I am certain that measures that seem utopian today may well seem politically possible and desirable after 50 years of pro-White policies.

The important thing is to begin now, while there is still a White majority and while we still have the freedom to speak and organize. Groups calling for an overthrow of the Constitution have always been subject to government infiltration and persecution, and in the age of the PATRIOT Act, things will only get worse.

Thus it is imperative for Whites to pursue their collective interests within the present political system and constitutional framework. (Fortunately, the Constitution contains provisions for its amendment.) As long as the First Amendment still has weight in the legal system, we must do everything we can within the law to advance our interests.

Revolutionary measures are legitimate only when a system prohibits peaceful change.

THE JEWISH QUESTION

My platform was criticized for being impractical and utopian for explicitly excluding Jews from the party and for advocating their removal from the United States. I hesitated some time over these proposals. But in the end, I decided that they are among the most fundamental practical proposals in the whole platform, fundamental because if these planks were removed, the whole party would be pointless.

The idea of admitting Jews to a party fighting against their interests is preposterous. Not that they wouldn't join. Indeed, they would join in large numbers if allowed. They would donate large sums of money. They would use their skills as persuaders, schemers, and swindlers to make themselves indispensable. They would rise rapidly to leadership positions.

Then they would sabotage the whole thing.

Any organization that does not explicitly exclude Jews will end up being dominated and subverted by them. No sense letting them put their noses under the tent.

That is why Jews have to leave America. They dominate the leading institutions of our culture: the political parties, the news and entertainment media, the arts, the education system, banking and finance. And they subvert these institutions to pursue Jewish interests at the expense of White interests. They are not the sole cause of America's problems, but they are a major cause, and there is no way to save this country without first taking them on.

I am not accusing Jews of "dual loyalties." There is no such thing. Whenever the allegedly dual objects of loyalty conflict, one wins out in the end. Whenever Jewish and American interests conflict, Jews invariably choose Jewish interests, and White Americans are left paying the bill, often with their lives.

Jews don't have dual loyalties, but they do have (officially or unofficially) "dual citizenships," and they take full advantage of them to exploit their host countries for Jewish advantage. Now that Jews have their own state, it is time to end the charade that they can be loyal citizens of anything other than the Jewish collective. I would be the biggest Zionist in the world if Jews would actually go to Israel. But they won't go as long as they can exploit dual citizenship status. A White People's Party would end that status and send them slouching towards Bethlehem.

"YOU CAN'T WIN."

In the long run, we'll have to win. But in the short run, yes, a White People's Party will suffer many electoral defeats. It is, however, a mistake to measure the success of a political party solely in terms of victories at the polls. A White People's Party can do a great deal of good even if it never wins an election.

First of all, a White People's Party will educate the public about how the system caters to Jews and non-Whites at the expense of the White majority.

Second, a White People's party, by standing frankly and unapologetically for White interests, will encourage and embolden White resistance to the multicultural society.

Third, to sustain itself through many electoral defeats, a White People's Party would have to become the nucleus for a new pro-White community. I caught a glimpse of such a community in September of 2001, when a generous friend made it possible for me to go to Paris to attend the *Fête des Bleu-Blanc-Rouge*, the annual rally of Jean-Marie Le Pen's *Front National*. There I saw thousands of French people of all ages, regions, classes, and walks of life drawn together to celebrate and defend who they are. Such community-building activities are valuable even if a party never wins an election.

In Paris with Paul Fromm and Jean-Marie Le Pen, September 2001

Fourth, a White People's Party may not win an election, but it can cause the Republicans to lose them. In a close race, if a White People's Party were to poll only one or two percent of the vote, it could defeat the Republicans. If the White People's Party were simultaneously to field candidates in close congressional districts across the nation, it could decimate the Republicans' congressional delegation. This would force the Republicans to cater to White voters in the next election cycle. If the Republicans fail to do so, the White People's Party will continue to grow, eventually to the point where it can win elections outright. Either way, Whites will benefit.

Regarding election strategies, I think that a White People's Party should begin by focusing on effecting change on the local and state level, trying to bypass the national government as much as possible. It seems to me, for instance, far more likely that a White People's Party could amend the Constitution through the state legislatures than through Congress.

"YOU CAN'T AVOID DIVISIVENESS."

I think that a White People's Party should adopt the strategy of shelving all political issues that divide Whites to pursue the most important issue of all: our survival.

But if party members are elected, they will be called upon to vote on many issues where Whites are divided. Would a White People's Party simply abstain from most political debates? Surely the voters would quickly find that intolerable. But the party could not allow its representative simply to vote their consciences either. It would have to take stands on divisive questions. Do we support limited government or pro-White social services? Do we support the environment if doing so conflicts with White workers' interests?

I think that this is an excellent objection, and I am not sure how to answer it. As I see it, the goal of a White People's party is not to answer or obviate all the political questions that divide Whites. Instead, it is to create a society in which all the political controversies that divide us remain live issues. It is just that the debates will be between Whites about what is best for Whites. If we could just bring that to pass, it would be progress enough for me.

"YOU'LL BE SMEARED AS NAZIS OR KLANSMEN."

The party I propose would not be affiliated with any other

pro-White group, including National Socialist and Klan groups. We would neither endorse nor condemn such groups, and we would gladly accept their support, as we would gladly accept the support of all pro-White individuals and organizations.

It is hard enough to persuade people that the White race is in danger and that Whites must rally to protect themselves. It would be harder still to combat more than a century of lies about the Civil War and Reconstruction, and more than half a century of lies about the Third Reich and World War II. Fortunately, it is not necessary.

But we'll still be smeared as Nazis and Klansmen. Our enemies will call us every name in the book. But, unlike conservative and libertarian cowards, we'll make no special effort to avoid or refute such smears. Such efforts are pointless, because our enemies will not be concerned with justice or accuracy. Besides, those who hesitate to defend ideas merely because they are shared by unfashionable individuals clearly lack courage and conviction.

Our standard response to all attempts to discredit us in the public mind by linking us to Nazis, the KKK, and other demonized groups would be: "To the extent that Nazis and Klansmen support our pro-White agenda, that is to their credit." We will never apologize for pursuing what is right and good.

"You'll be smeared as racists."

Of course we will. We are racists. But we do not regard this as a smear, but as a badge of honor. Race is real. Different races are genetically capable of different ways of life, just as different breeds of dog are genetically capable of different ways of life. American civilization cannot be maintained by replacing Whites with non-Whites anymore than poodles can replace sheepdogs and chihuahuas can replace sled dogs. Racism is an objective and enlightened viewpoint, and we will not apologize for it.

"You'll be smeared as White Supremacists."

Again, this is no smear, but a badge of honor. America ruled by and for Whites was a great nation. America ruled by and for Jews and non-Whites is a nation in decline. A White People's

Party will restore American greatness by restoring, perfecting, and perpetuating White supremacy.

"BUT WHAT ABOUT THE NON-WHITES?"

I was genuinely surprised to receive this question. In my eyes, there is no honor and no credit in concerning oneself with the interests of other races. They can look out for themselves. The White People's Party is not interested in non-Whites and Jews. They have the Democratic party, the Republican party, the Libertarian party, the Reform party, and every other institution in our society looking out for their interests. We are interested only in looking out for White people. That's the whole point.

November 23, 2003

My Awakening Too*

Thank you, ladies and gentlemen.

I am honored to have the opportunity to address this group of patriots and to offer suggestions for the future of our cause. I also want to offer special thanks to my friend Sam Dickson for making it possible for me to be here.

Above all, I would like to thank David Duke. It is easy for me to discuss David Duke and strategies that work to promote the White cause in the same speech, for a very simple reason: Duke works.

There are people here who can talk with far greater authority than I about what works in the areas of policy options and campaign strategies, so I am going to focus on my personal experiences.

David Duke's *My Awakening* was my awakening, too. I read it in the Spring of 1999, in my Freshman year at Emory University. Emory had rolled out a red carpet for me. I was one of 20 recipients in my class of the school's most prestigious academic scholarship. My future was all mapped out. I would study biology, get good grades, compete on the swim team, go to a top medical school, and have a lucrative career.

But Emory was teaching lies: the lie of racial equality; the lie that the differences between the races and the sexes are not based in nature, but are mere social constructs that can be changed with sufficient coercion and brainwashing; the lie that multiculturalism leads to utopia not oblivion; the lie that the White race is a cancer on the planet rather than nature's fairest, noblest, most creative species.

Emory was teaching lies, and I could not ignore it. I started searching for truth. I had heard of David Duke when I was 12 years old, and I knew he was unafraid to advocate politically incorrect ideas. I credit *My Awakening* for articulating, affirming,

---

* This is the text of the speech I delivered at the International European American Unity and Leadership Conference held in New Orleans, Memorial Day weekend, 2004.

and supporting what I already suspected about race, for introducing me entirely to the Jewish role in suppressing racial truths and corrupting our politics and culture, and *most importantly,* for convincing me of the need to *act.*

Mr. Duke convinced me not only with his clear style and impressive command of facts. I also found his personality appealing. He confounded the negative media stereotypes. He struck me as idealistic, sincere, principled, and brave. He struck me as compassionate and broad-minded. And, most importantly, he made it clear that his primary motivation was love of his own people, not hatred of others.

These impressions were confirmed when I first met Mr. Duke at a rally in support of the Confederate Flag on top of the South Carolina Capitol. Duke delivered a great speech about the need to actively resist attempts to destroy our heritage as White Americans. Nowhere in his speech, however, did he say anything hateful towards other races. I was convinced that Mr. Duke was taking the high road to our racial salvation, and that was the road I would like to follow.

During the spring of my sophomore year at Emory (i.e., Spring 2000), the President of the University declared the upcoming 2000–2001 school year to be the all-encompassing "Year of Reconciliation." Its organizers encouraged student and faculty participation, and made it clear that reconciliation requires diverse viewpoints to be expressed. I saw this as an excellent opportunity to publicly challenge the dogma of racial egalitarianism and encourage its "reconciliation" with the massive and continually-increasing scientific and empirical evidence to the contrary.

I decided that I needed a platform, so I approached the student paper, *The Emory Wheel,* and was allowed to write a regular column. On October 6th, 2000, I published an editorial with the very cautious title "Genes May Determine Racial Attributes." I cited UC-Berkeley Professor Emeritus Arthur Jensen's magisterial 1998 book *The g Factor,* which offers the most powerful case yet for the thesis that intelligence is primarily a matter of genetics and that the races differ considerably in their intelligence. Since genes cannot be altered by social policy, I questioned the wisdom of such programs as affirmative action and head-start.

Then all hell broke loose. Virtually the entire university, from the President on down, attacked me. The President wrote an open letter condemning me in the next issue of the *Wheel*, and there was a protest march as well as a public forum—more of a Stalinist-style show trial, really—where I was given five minutes to defend my views against a tag team of six professors.

That editorial was the beginning of my commitment to becoming a public voice, a public fighter for our cause. And I probably would not have done it if I had not read *My Awakening*.

I want to compare Duke's approach to that taken by another great man who also played a significant role in my awakening: the late Dr. William Pierce.

With William Pierce and Hadley, Hillsboro, W.Va., July 2001

I first encountered Dr. Pierce through his American Dissident Voices broadcasts available through the National Alliance website. I was impressed by Pierce's scientific mind, his command of facts, and his ability to dissect the falsehoods told by mainstream politicians of both parties. His name aptly depicted his ability to cut through lies and obfuscations and get to the truth.

At the end of my sophomore year, as I was planning my campaign for the Year of Reconciliation, I drove up to Hillsboro, West Virginia, to meet with Dr. Pierce. I was surprised to find that he was a warm, jovial, laid-back, fatherly fellow.

I was surprised, not because of what the mass media had told me, but because of what Pierce himself had told me. For along with his facts and analysis, his on-air personality was gruff and angry, and he was given to sharing homicidal fantasies. Indeed, he wrote two novels filled with them.

I wound up having pizza with Pierce and Victor Gerhard, a lawyer who volunteered his services for the National Alliance. We ate in Pierce's home up the hill from his office, so I had the opportunity to meet all of Pierce's cats, not just Hadley. Although I love animals, I am somewhat allergic to cats, particularly if I happen to rub my eyes after petting them, a mistake I made that evening.

Dr. Pierce saw that I was having an allergic reaction. He told me he had some generic Claritin, got up from the table, and returned with three or four small unmarked pills. He said that since I have a muscular build, I should take them all, and handed them to me.

I remember recalling the scene in *The Matrix*, where Neo is given the choice between a pill that will awaken him and bring him into the real world, and a pill that will cause him to go back to the dream world of the matrix. In a way, I was facing a similar choice.

Until then I would never have taken pills from someone I had just met, particularly unmarked pills. But there I was, in unfamiliar territory, with two men I had only just met, at the national headquarters of an organization the mainstream media would have us believe is pure evil. In a very real way I felt like I was entrusting my entire future to Pierce by swallowing those pills.

But swallow them I did. To my everlasting relief, my allergy symptoms disappeared shortly thereafter. The doctor had cured me. I consider that to be the moment I lost any desire to be a "respectable conservative" and started thinking of myself as a full-fledged radical.

I visited Dr. Pierce a second time in the summer of 2001. Something he said then will stick with me always. He told me that giving up his career in science was the hardest thing he ever did. But once he did it, he had no regrets because nothing compares with the freedom to spend your entire life speaking the truth as you see it.

I admired Dr. Pierce immensely, and I lamented his untimely death. But I feel that he could have been even more effective if he had kept his dark side in check. Now I am no pacifist. There may come a day when we have to fight for our survival by whatever means necessary. But I don't enjoy thinking about such eventualities, and I wonder if Dr. Pierce did.

The persona you project will attract similar people and repel dissimilar people. By airing his fantasies about violence, Dr. Pierce repelled many high-quality people who could not see behind the mask, but he appealed to homicidal misfits like Timothy McVeigh, an antiracist whose accomplice Terry Nichols married a non-White—a man who apparently learned nothing from *The Turner Diaries* but how to make a truck bomb.

We have to remember that we're fighting for what is true and good, that we are the enlightened ones, we are the educated ones, we occupy the moral high ground. And we have to act the part. Like David Duke. We can't afford to give our people the false impression that we are cat-coddling villains from James Bond movies out to exterminate nine-tenths of the planet's featherless bipeds.

I believe that what prevents many thinking White men and women from supporting the movement isn't that we lack a factual basis for our beliefs. They hold back because, on a deep subconscious level, they've been conditioned to believe that the truth is *evil*.

It sounds crazy, but it's true. I know I myself hesitated before read-ing the section of *My Awakening* that deals with the Jewish Ques-tion. I was amazed to discover that somehow I had been brain-washed to think that simply criticizing Jews was evil. Fortunately, my rational side prevailed. But it probably would not have pre-vailed if I had not, by that time, formed a positive impression of Duke's character. That is what carried me through.

Politics is a matter of appearances. It is not enough to *be* right. You have to *seem* right too. It is not enough to *be* good. You have to *seem* good too. The kind of persona you project will determine the kind of people who follow you. That is why it is so important to stay on the high road.

One final thought: David Duke has proved that it's *actually possible* for a racialist candidate to succeed in America. And the Republican Party adopted — or at least paid lip-service to — many of Duke's proposals after he achieved public office, most notably his anti-Affirmative Action positions. They did this not because they wanted to do the right thing, but rather because they simp-ly could not afford to lose racialist votes.

I would like to see Duke get back into active campaigning. A while back, I wrote an article entitled "A Party of Our Own" which outlined a basic platform and strategy for a political party aimed at protecting White interests in the multiracial society America has become. A White Party would not always be able to elect candidates — although Duke proves that it is possible — but it could consistently accomplish two important goals. First, it would be a vehicle for getting the truth out. Second, if a White Party were to run candidates in close districts, it could easily pull enough votes away from the Republicans to defeat them. Then the Republicans would have to choose between Jewish money and racialist votes. A White Party is a heads we win, tails they lose strategy. And with Duke on the loose, it might just happen.

There's so much that can be done. Let's start doing it.

It's been a real honor. Thank you once again.

May 30, 2004

MOTIVATION

A few days ago I had a telephone conversation with a friend and lifelong racial activist, Sam Dickson. We shared opinions on several matters, both personal and movement-related. Near the end of the conversation, however, he confided in me a deep sense of hopelessness and despair. Having spent decades of his life fighting for the "Cause," he found himself having serious doubts about its ultimate success. All I could say at the time was, "Don't give up."

I felt more was needed, however. I myself have gotten depressed while thinking about the future of our country and our race, and I have allowed these feelings to interfere with my productivity. I have also felt an acute sense of guilt for having produced nothing new over the past few months. Hence, this essay.

Generally speaking, one's effectiveness at any endeavor depends to a large extent on one's enthusiasm and confidence of success. I have come to believe that enthusiasm and motivation are more important than talent in determining success: I've seen plenty of motivated idiots who have achieved fortune and fame, but absolutely no unmotivated geniuses who have done so.

Motivation is literally the force that moves us forward. It is thus the lifeblood of any endeavor. Indeed, it is life itself. And negative thinking, and the depression to which it ultimately leads, are therefore enemies of life. Depression is a kind of living death. That's why the severely depressed often prefer death to life.

What if Beethoven, upon becoming deaf, became depressed and lost all motivation to complete his Ninth Symphony? What if Galileo had convinced himself that the Church was too great a force to challenge? Think about what the world would be like absent the accomplishments of any great explorer, discoverer, writer, or artist.

Humanity would be poorer without the works of any great individual. Yet in spite of the loss, more great accomplishments would eventually occur, provided future generations have the genetic background they need.

If present trends continue, they will not.

The greatest accomplishment our race could ever make is to ensure that future generations of our people will exist and prosper. Individuals and groups who effectively act with that goal in mind are engaging in the highest and noblest activity possible.

I think many high-quality White Nationalists accept this idea, yet still hold back from fully committing themselves to the movement for one reason or another. I think the greatest unspoken feeling is: "If we were going to win, we would have won already. White Nationalist leaders have been addressing the threat to our race for a long time, but the results have been insignificant, and America continues to decline. I don't feel I could make any difference, so why should I try?"

I admit to having entertained these thoughts myself. But when I took the time to rationally consider the argument, its flaws became obvious.

First of all, past events do not dictate what will happen in the future. The probability a normal coin will come up "heads" after being flipped is 50:50, even if the coin came up "tails" the past 1,000 flips. The fact that Da Vinci was unsuccessful at creating a flying machine didn't stop the Wright Brothers from doing so.

The lessons of history are important, but the most important of these lessons is that history is full of surprises, novelties, and new discoveries. And by their very nature, these things cannot be predicted in advance, for if they could be predicted, they would not be new, novel, or surprising. History tells us only that we will be surprised, not what the surprises will be.

Second, even if one's message is absolutely true and good, it will be ineffective unless certain other conditions are met. One needs the appropriate media for communicating it. One's audience has to be receptive. And one needs the right spokesmen for the message. And as I see it, the prospects for all three of these conditions are positive.

First, although the establishment has had near total control over public opinion for a long time through the mass media, their grip is weakening. Consider the following. In the past decade: (1) Internet access has become standard in most American households. (2) Digital media such as the CD and the DVD have all but replaced analog media. (3) The computing power needed to capture and manipulate digital photography and digital video has become affordable to the average consumer. (4) File-sharing technologies have emerged that allow for the rapid distribution of large amounts of data to a large number of interested parties. Thus the technical barriers to forming a truly independent media have all but disappeared. All that's needed now is time, determined effort, and a bit of creativity.

Second, as things go from bad to worse in America, more and more people are becoming receptive to alternative arguments, even if those arguments do not conform to the tenets of Political Correctness. This is particularly true among young people who have grown up exposed to the internet, where any topic they wish to explore is but a Google search away. At the same time, our ability to communicate the truth becomes greater and greater with each passing day. These facts should inspire us to speak out louder and more vigorously than ever before.

Third, since I started this website, I have been contacted by hundreds of people. Many have shared their criticisms of today's White Nationalist leaders. I have noticed that the strongest objections have come from the people who have the most to offer the movement in terms of leadership and money. They are educated, affluent, talented, individually reputable, and socially prominent people.

When I have urged such people to get publicly involved themselves if they do not like the existing leadership, they tend to answer that they cannot, because they have so much to lose. They are worried about the consequences to their families, their businesses, their personal reputations, and their social status.

My standard answer to this sort of objection is: Having a family is the best reason in the world to fight for a society where White children have a future. Preserving one's wealth and social status are excellent reasons for fighting as well. If one really does have a good reputation, then why worry about it being sullied by the advocacy of politically incorrect truths? Indeed, if one's reputation really is good, then won't it lend luster to unfairly tarnished truths, rather than vice versa?

The first step toward victory is believing that it is possible.

September 6, 2004

MEET, EAT, & MOVE FORWARD

In the spring of 1999, during my Freshman year at Emory University I received a package. I knew it contained a copy of David Duke's *My Awakening*, which I had purchased off Amazon.com a week or so earlier. Before opening it, I made sure I was alone in my dorm room, because of the oppressive atmosphere of Political Correctness on campus.

Earlier that year, a friend had been kicked out of his dormitory for jokingly teasing his roommate (also a friend of mine) by putting up a picture of two attractive women outside their room with a dialog box saying "Too bad you're gay, S—." The lesbian couple in charge of the hall saw it, took offense, reported it, and after a "hearing" my friend was barred from university housing. The reason cited was that his actions "created an uncomfortable environment for gays and lesbians."

Of course nobody cared that the whole affair created an uncomfortable environment for me and anyone else with politically incorrect thoughts: That was the whole point. Thus I knew I had to be extremely careful while exploring the race question to avoid the same fate.

Once alone, I ripped open the package like a child at Christmas. I quickly examined the contents of the book and immediately knew I was in for a good read. Yet oddly enough, I hesitated to begin. I wondered if I was committing a great evil by even daring to consider "racist" and "anti-Semitic" ideas. I dismissed this thought as wildly irrational, but even then I took great care to insure no one else knew what I was reading. I felt that I would be shunned and denounced, even by close friends, for displaying an interest in alternative viewpoints.

Shortly after my column on race, IQ, and crime appeared during my Junior year, I was contacted by several local sympathizers who saw the coverage of the race forum on the local news. When I arranged to meet with one, a lawyer and longtime racial activist, I was still extremely cautious about how I treated the race/intelligence issue, being accustomed to the scripted disgust showed by many at Emory at the very suggestion that racial differences in intelligence have a genetic origin. So I avoided discussion of the political and social implications of Arthur Jensen's research, sticking instead to defending it on its scientific merit.

After talking for several minutes, it became clear that my concern was unfounded, for this man spoke frankly about not only race, but also about political issues like Duke's campaigns for public office in Louisiana, as well as the Jewish question. I can't describe how exhilarated I felt when I learned I could speak with complete frankness with my soon-to-be friend.

I had, of course, discussed these issues with people online, and I had even met some like-minded people in person about an hour outside of Atlanta. But I never knew anyone who lived close by who shared my views on racial matters, and unconsciously I thought everywhere within a ten mile radius of Emory was hostile territory as far as the truth about race was concerned.

It's amazing that such brainwashing and intimidation can occur in a supposedly free country, but I'm certain many readers can readily identify with how I felt during my path to racial awareness, and the feeling of liberation upon finding like-minded others.

The benefits of establishing face-to-face communities are many: friendship, education, networking, etc. Above all, however, is the psychological benefit of having one's own heartfelt beliefs affirmed by others.

Even independent thinkers can benefit from such affirmation, since no one enjoys social isolation. Regardless of how logical and well-considered one's opinions are, if one is alone in holding them one feels unfulfilled on a deep subconscious level. At best, such feelings fester into misanthropy. At worst, they lead to depression. I have experienced both, and neither is healthy.

It is relatively easy to establish a network of like-minded friends through online message boards and instant messenger services. Such virtual communities can be helpful for discussing ideas and feeling somewhat less alienated. Online contacts can also be a prelude to in-person encounters, especially when discovering people who live close by.

But all things equal, online friends are a poor substitute for real-world friends. Until one meets online friends in person, one always wonders if they are for real. Shared ideas are only one part of friendship, and the other character traits that play a role cannot be easily discerned through a computer screen.

The Atlanta lawyer I met introduced me to a group he referred to as the "Tuesday Night Club." Jokingly, he called it the "Hate Group." The group met weekly in a private dining room at a local restaurant. Typically between 5 and 20 people showed up. They were a rather impressive group. All of them were well-read, well-spoken, and deeply concerned about our race and its problems. Most of them were remarkably accomplished as well. There were a number of lawyers, several successful businessmen, a doctor, a couple of Ph.D.s, and so forth. Although there were lively differences of opinion, all agreed on the basics of racial difference and on the need for radical change in public policy.

The Tuesday Night Club was not an activist group, although many of its members are very active in the pro-White cause. Instead, it was what Tom Metzger satirizes as a "meet, eat, and retreat" group. Primarily we just talked. Usually the appointed "Hate Master" would pose a question to mull over while we read the menu and enjoyed side conversations. Then, after the food appeared, we would go around the table and each person would give his or her take on the topic.

Sometimes the meetings were depressing. Admit it: there is a lot to be depressed about. But I always came away better informed and with new and often improved perspectives. The meetings also served to radicalize more moderate individuals who see America's racial problems but aren't sure what to do about them. I also appreciated the chance to practice my public speaking in front of a friendly audience. And, on a deeper psychological level, all the meetings were positive just because they were a genuine, face-to-face community.

I admire the hard work and dedication of those who have created virtual White communities on the internet, through news sites, broadcasts, and discussion forums. But I would like to encourage Whites to take the next step: forming face-to-face communities, and a weekly dinner and discussion group is an excellent model to follow.

November 30, 2003

REAL HISTORY,
REAL COMMUNITY

In the previous chapter, I wrote about the need to form real, face-to-face White communities, and I offered as one model the Tuesday evening dinner and discussion group that I attended in Atlanta. On Thursday, December 11th in San Francisco, I had another taste of White community. Historian David Irving, whose fame makes any introduction unnecessary, spoke to a group of 34 people after dinner at a German restaurant.

When I entered the meeting room, I was a bit taken aback at what I thought was *Triumph of the Will* playing on a large-screen TV. Mr. Irving greeted me warmly with a handshake and explained that what we were seeing was actually *Victory of Faith*, Leni Riefenstahl's long-lost prequel to *Triumph of the Will*. Hitler had ordered all copies destroyed after the purge of Ernst Röhm, who appears prominently in the film. Riefenstahl went to her death hoping that a copy would come to light one day, and when one turned up recently in England it was quickly released on VHS and DVD.

Mr. Irving offered copies of *Victory of Faith* for sale, along with copies of his most recent two books, *Churchill's War*, vol. II, and the most recent edition of *Hitler's War*, the new Hungarian translation of *Uprising!*, and some extremely beautiful historical picture books published in Germany by Arndt Verlag.

Hitler's War and *Churchill's War*, vol. II, are not only splendidly written, they are also splendidly produced: tastefully designed, loaded with gorgeous photographs, and printed to the highest standards of quality. Another way Irving's Focal Point imprint puts mainstream publishers to shame is his astonishingly generous offer of free downloads of all his books, so you can read them before you decide to buy them.

Mr. Irving was quite generous with his autograph. Not only does he autograph the books he sells on the spot, he invites his audience to bring in other David Irving titles to sign. He was even a good sport about somebody's request to autograph a book by another author!

The talk itself dealt with parallels between Gulf War II and World War II. Of course the warmongers and their apologists love to draw parallels between Iraq and Nazi Germany, casting Saddam as Hitler, just as the Clinton regime cast Milosevic as Hitler when they wanted to attack Serbia. The fact that the US government — including such members of the Bush regime as Cheney and Rumsfeld — saw fit to do business with Saddam in the past, poses a dilemma. Either Saddam really isn't another Hitler, or Cheney and Rumsfeld are willing to deal with another Hitler. Either way, the Bush regime looks bad.

With David Irving, Thursday, December 11, 2003, in San Francisco

But this is a war for Jews, so Bush can trust the Jew-controlled media not to raise such questions. Instead, they show us images of the "liberation" of Baghdad staged to look like the "liberation" of Paris. The "Coalition," just like the "Allies," triumphs over an "Axis" of evil and sets up "democracy" — i.e., a sham democracy that does not let certain parties to compete for election. And Jews live happily ever after on the spoils.

Irving's talk completely reversed the analogies between the two wars, casting the US as Nazi Germany and Iraq as Soviet Russia, and told a depressingly familiar tale of imperialism, arrogance, and bad planning coming to grief against partisan warfare conducted by a well-armed, fanatical populace. It is a tale that does not have a happy ending for the US.

David Irving is a remarkably eloquent speaker. He is also reputed to be surly, abrasive, and bitter. Frankly, given the amount of persecution he has endured at the instigation of Jews around the world, he would have every right to be. But in San Francisco he was nothing but warm and gracious. He handled the questions after his talk quite well, and I was pleased to hear that he is now researching a biography of Heinrich Himmler.

Irving was also quite funny. A few lines stuck in my mind. He remarked that in many ways he actually preferred *Victory of Faith* to *Triumph of the Will* because it is looser and more "slap happy." When he referred to the country of Niger, he promised to refer to it as "the 'N' country" to avoid giving any possible offense. Regarding the planned HBO dramatization of the Lipstadt libel trial, he expressed pleasure at being played by Anthony Hopkins, "because I like eating human flesh too." He also lamented that Rock Hudson isn't around to play Deborah Lipstadt.

An important part of the event was the opportunity to meet people with common interests. Most in the audience were White males, as is usual with these sorts of groups, but there were some women. Ages ranged from late teens to gray heads. Most looked conservative, but there were also beards, ponytails, and John Lennon glasses.

Although I suppose some might merely have been WW II buffs, and one man had an Oriental wife, the people I met were all White Nationalists. There were several professionals, a college professor, a publisher, and a self-described blue collar man. All of them were well-informed and well-spoken, and it was a real pleasure to be among people who understood and would not mince words about our race's perilous situation.

At the San Francisco event, I was pleased to hear talk of

forming a weekly dinner and discussion group on the Atlanta model. There is no reason why such groups could not spring up in every city Mr. Irving visits.

David Irving offers two increasingly rare commodities to today's White Nationalist: real history and real community. Seek him out.

December 13, 2003

WHAT WE CAN LEARN
FROM LEFTISTS

Last night I attended a screening of *We Interrupt This Empire*, a documentary video presented as a fundraising event for anti-FTAA activists on the University of California, Berkeley campus. (The "FTAA" refers to the "Free Trade Area of the Americas," a proposal that would extend NAFTA to cover the western hemisphere.) The video covers the massive protests that occurred in San Francisco the day after bombing in Iraq commenced, the so-called "direct action" protests designed to shut down the major corporations for a day.

The documentary not only does an excellent job at informing its audience of the relevant facts, it also instills in viewers a spirit of rebellion, a sense that acting *directly* against an unjust system is the way to go. The video highlights the underground wheeling-and-dealing and insider bartering between the corporate leaders and politicians who direct our foreign policy.

It shows a clip I have never seen, even once, on the mainstream media: Donald Rumsfeld shaking hands with Saddam Hussein in the early 1980s, back when Hussein posed no threat to US economic interests.

It shows how all the major media networks fell in line to support the war, giving the hundred or so pro-war marchers in Washington almost as much coverage as was given to the hundreds of thousands who marched in San Francisco.

It shows Bush's vacuous, simian countenance attempting a look of genuine gravity and profundity the night the bombing started.

It accurately depicts the misguided "patriots" who naïvely believe what they're told to believe. It interviews Muslims who have been affected by the PATRIOT act, and it reveals Ashcroft's smirk as he's asked a question regarding a change in the national mood ring color from yellow to orange.

It shows the capitalist system at its worst, though its worst is the only conceivable outcome after all feelings of higher loyalty to the environment and to one's race and culture have been re-moved. Yet it also shows people taking their anger and striking back against the system.

Most of my life I'd considered myself a conservative, and had thus viewed New Age types, long-haired hippies, and pot-smoking activists with suspicion, and rightfully so. Many have character flaws as well as unrealistic, unnatural attitudes about how the world works. I had always assumed most of them dressed and acted as they do simply to spite their parents or to rebel in an "approved" way, a way that doesn't truly address what's wrong with the country.

Yet my opinion has changed over the past few years. I underestimated the general intelligence of most of them, and I've discovered that many can argue quite articulately for why America's "war on drugs" or the "war on terror" should be ended.

Of course, I will never become one. Nearly all tote politically correct ideas about race, and few are willing to admit *any* genetically based, immutable differences in ability between individuals. Thus their socialist visions would spell disaster for America.

Yet those of us who are not as naïve about race have much to learn from these leftists. We need to emulate their level of social activism and their ability to organize and protest effectively.

More importantly, we need to get our message out using every resource available to us, as they do. *We Interrupt This Empire* left me feeling invigorated and inspired, and wanting to participate in future protests. It expresses a revolutionary spirit more and more people are beginning to share, a spirit of outrage and contempt for the self-serving oligarchy that rules this country. It shows people justifiably enraged at the fact they've lost control over their government. And it shows them defying authority to oppose it.

I'm convinced of the power of video to deliver a compelling message that affects the viewer on an emotional level as well as an intellectual one. It's now time to design documentary videos that expose America's racial disparities in graphic, sensual detail.

No technological impediments stop us from achieving this goal. Sophisticated editing that used to require expensive, specialized equipment can now be done on a personal computer. The number of people who have high-speed internet connections capable of high-quality streaming video will increase exponentially in the next several years. In the future many satellite and broadband cable TV networks will be "wired," and viewing a website will be as easy as switching a channel . . .

In other words, the dominoes are all lined up. All we need to do is act.

October 24, 2003

SEX DIFFERENCES

A few days ago I had a heated discussion about sex differences with a female friend of mine who calls herself a feminist. She agrees with me that races differ on a variety of traits and that genetics play a large role in shaping these differences. Yet she found it impossible to believe that behavioral differences between the sexes might also have a genetic basis rather than a cultural one.

She began by decrying "sexism," which she sees as ubiquitous in American culture (and even worse in many European cultures.) As evidence, she pointed out that nearly all mainstream advertisements use women, rather than men, for sex-appeal. She finds such advertising "degrading to women" and asked "why don't they use men just as much?" She expressed the opinion that society teaches men to treat women as sex objects through such advertising, saying "it's no wonder such men hit their wives when they get married." She also expressed a belief that societal expectations and traditional gender roles were "sexist" as well, holding women back from achieving their potential. She used the fact that women are underrepresented in certain fields as evidence of gender discrimination and "sexism" at work, calling me "sexist" to think otherwise.

The more she continued, the more bellicose she became. After mentioning domestic abuse, she remarked, "I'd hit back if that ever happened to me." Then she looked at me in the eye with a fiery glare and said, "You think women can't fight?" She then expressed a dangerous and destructive feminist sentiment: "When cloning becomes available, women won't need men. We could let men die off if we wanted. We'll be able to take care of ourselves."

It would be otiose to pick apart the logical flaws in her reasoning about sexism, since they essentially mirror the flaws made by those who decry racism in society. Her main premise, namely, that biology has nothing to do with observed differences in gender representation, is untenable given what science knows about sex. Yet her statement about cloning provoked me to consider sex differences further: specifically, their origins, their future, and how society should deal with sex and sex differences.

Evolutionarily speaking, it's not clear at first why sex arose in the first place. Searching for a mate takes time and energy, and may increase the searcher's risk of being killed by a predator. Once found, a potential mate may demand additional exertion or investment before agreeing to cooperate. Sex itself may expose the parties to sexually transmitted diseases. And after all that, the mating may prove to be infertile. Why not avoid all the trouble and risk, and simply reproduce asexually instead?

The current prevailing view of why sex came about is called the "Red Queen hypothesis." It holds that sex arose as a result of a host/parasite "arms race": hosts (usually larger, more complex organisms) have to continually adapt to prevent parasites (usually smaller, single-celled organisms or viruses) from targeting a specific genotype.

Sex allows for genotypic variation between parent and child, since children are genetically distinct from their parents and from one another (except in the case of identical twins). If we reproduced asexually, and had families comprised of identical individuals (barring chance genetic mutations), then a parasite that could kill one member of the family would kill the others just as rapidly. If humanity were comprised of merely large families comprised of identical individuals, then parasites would have a much easier job.

So why do the sexes differ with regard to size, appearance, and behavior, not only among humans but among every other sexually reproducing organism? Sexual reproduction places very different selection pressures on females versus males. Simply put, eggs (or pregnancies) are more expensive than ejaculates. In more general terms, females typically make a larger parental investment in each offspring than do males. "Parental investment" refers to the time and energy expended in creating and caring for offspring. Parental investment increases the reproductive success of a particular offspring while simultaneously decreasing the parent's future reproductive successes.

In more than 90% of mammalian species, females provide substantial parental care and males provide none whatsoever.

One extreme example is the orangutan. After a brief tryst, including about 15 minutes of copulation, the male and female go their separate ways. If a pregnancy results, the mother will carry the fetus for eight months, give birth, and nurse and protect the baby for about seven or eight years. For the father, on the other hand, the beginning and end of parental investment is a few grams of semen.

Sex differences came about as a result of these differing demands. A female's potential reproductive success is relatively small, and is limited more by the number of eggs she can make (or pregnancies she can carry) than by the number of males she can convince to mate with her. In contrast, a male's potential reproductive success is relatively large, and is limited more by the number of females he can convince to mate with him than by the number of ejaculates he can make.

These facts allow predictions about differences in the mating behavior of the two sexes:

Males should be competitive. If the reproductive success of males is limited by access to females, then we expect males will compete among themselves for opportunities to mate.

Females should be choosy. If the reproductive success of females is not limited by opportunities to mate, but any given mating may involve the commitment of the female to a large investment in offspring, females should be selective about with whom they mate.

The competitiveness of males and the choosiness of females have manifested themselves in the physical and behavioral differences between the sexes. That advertisers choose to use women rather than men in sex-appeal advertising is no surprise: women, being choosier than men, aren't as responsive to pictures of attractive men as men are to pictures of attractive women. Advertisers simply do what sells.

Sex has been around for far, far longer than the 140,000 or so years human races have. That people still argue that behavioral differences between men and women result purely from cultural influences (or that such a belief ever arose in the first place, given the ubiquity of sex and sex differences in the animal kingdom) highlights just how irrational some so-called "progressive intellectuals" can be.

On a closing note, it's worth noting that the sexes are designed to complement one another, both physically and mentally. Humanity is only half complete with one or the other missing. Thus, it's nonsense to talk of one sex being superior to another: Each has qualities the other lacks. Discord between the sexes stems from a lack of proper understanding and respect for these differences. Since sex is and will probably always be the simplest, cheapest, and most pleasurable form of reproduction, such discord (seen far more among Whites than any other race, and far more among the more intelligent than the less) can only hurt the future of the race.

October 21, 2003

WOMEN & WHITE NATIONALISM

White Nationalist groups are almost exclusively men's clubs, and most of the men are bachelors who complain that they cannot find suitable women. Furthermore, those men who are married frequently complain that their wives are indifferent or even hostile to their views about race. Men, it seems, are far more willing to espouse politically incorrect views about race than women. After perusing various websites and forums discussing this topic, I've found that many men resent this fact, construing it as some sort of moral failing on the part of women. But it is not. It merely reflects the hard-wired biological differences between the sexes.

Sex places different pressures on males and females. Eggs take more energy to produce than sperm, and females alone have to bear a pregnancy. And in over 90% of mammalian species, females provide substantial parental care while males provide none whatsoever. Thus females make a much larger parental investment in each offspring than do males. Parental investment increases the reproductive success of the offspring receiving it, while simultaneously decreasing the parent's future reproductive success by consuming resources that could be spent on additional offspring.

Differences in behavior between the sexes came about as a result of these differing demands. A female's potential reproductive success is relatively small, and is limited more by the number of eggs she can produce (or pregnancies she can carry) than by the number of males she can convince to mate with her. In contrast, a male's potential reproductive success is relatively large, and is limited more by the number of females he can convince to mate with him than by the number of sperm he can produce. This difference in potential reproductive success allows us to predict that males will compete with each other for access to mates, while females will be selective about with whom they mate. Sexually, males are adventurers and risk-takers, while females are risk-avoiders.

These differences in reproductive strategies go beyond sex. The competitiveness of males drives them to take risks more frequently, not just when appealing to females, but also in day-to-day decision-making. Car insurance rates are higher for teenage boys than for girls for precisely this reason. Risk-taking "raises the stakes" of many decisions, increasing the potential rewards but also increasing the consequences of failure.

This risk-taking makes evolutionary sense, because males are far more expendable than females. If all women were killed except one, the race would take many generations to return to its original size, if ever. Yet if all the men were killed except one, the remaining man would have his work cut out for him, but the race could theoretically repopulate within a generation. Since males are not as necessary for the maintenance of population size, males tend to take more risks, be more aggressive, and tend to work towards establishing themselves higher in social hierarchies than do women.

But if women are inherently conservative, then why are they generally more supportive of left-wing causes than men? First of all, in spite of the leftist rhetoric about progress and radical change, the leftist emphasis on social welfare, social planning, and anti-competitive egalitarianism has an obvious appeal to risk-averse females. Furthermore, in spite of the leftist posture of always being outsiders, the left now controls most of the authoritative institutions of society: the educational system, the news and entertainment media, the churches, etc. Leftist opinion is the *status quo*. Women are brainwashed to accept it and loath to criticize it, for fear of the risks to their social standing, their employment, and especially to the well-being of their children.

But more women support the White racialist movement now than in the past. I know this from personal experience. I have been reading racialist-oriented USENET newsgroups (and web-based bulletin boards, once the technology was developed), ever since I first went "online" back in 1994 or 1995. I posted a personals ad on Stormfront years ago, shortly after the personals section was created. I didn't receive any responses. I did the same thing just several months ago, and was contacted by a number of women.

Part of the reason may be that women are more comfortable expressing politically incorrect ideas anonymously on the internet, a far less risky prospect than espousing the same views openly.

But surely that is not the main reason. For the same reason that women have been slow to take up the White nationalist cause, women may eventually become its strongest and most uncompromising supporters: their maternal instincts. More women are joining the White nationalist cause as it becomes increasingly evident that the health and welfare of future generations of Whites is at stake.

Aside from the love and protection my own mother gave me (which continues to this day), my first encounter with female maternal instinct came when I was seven or eight years old. At a lake near my old school, I observed a mallard duck leading her ducklings. Curious boy that I was, I ran over to the ducklings and picked one up. Although most adult ducks at the lake were apprehensive about approaching humans even when they were sharing food, the mother turned, came right up to me, and started quacking loudly. When I knelt down, she proceeded to flog my arm with her wing until I released the duckling. I was shocked at the length to which this mother would go to protect her baby. She went from risk aversion to quite possibly risking her life, but the underlying biological imperative was the same.

I have the feeling that more White mothers will begin behaving like that mother duck, once they can no longer ignore the fact that the world their children will inherit will be worse than the one into which they were born. In the meantime, more individuals need to stick their necks out, especially young men. Future generations of our race are counting on us.

November 4, 2003

STRONG WOMEN

"You're just afraid of strong women!" I can't count the number of times I have heard this accusation hurled at men who break up with their girlfriends after tiring of their feminist posturing and antics.

I confess: I *am* afraid of "strong women." There are good reasons to dislike and even to fear them.

Let's examine today's definition of "strong women." "Strong women" are not those who can lift heavy objects, carry baskets on their heads, and so forth. "Strong women" are not those who can bear with dignity the sorrows of life and death. "Strong women" are not those who, in addition to the burdens of motherhood, heroically shoulder the responsibilities of dead, dysfunctional, divorced, or otherwise absent fathers.

No, what is meant by "strong women" today is: women who can do anything and everything a man can do, just as well or even better, and so do not need men. As the saying goes, a "strong woman" needs a man like a fish needs a bicycle. (Surely this is one of the dumbest and ugliest analogies ever to attain the lofty status of cliché.)

But it is nice to be needed: needed emotionally, not just for physical tasks like taking out the trash, squashing spiders, and manhandling recalcitrant jar lids. What man in his right mind would prefer a woman who doesn't need him to a woman who does? The only man who prefers a woman who doesn't need him doesn't really need her either. She may be useful to him for a while, for sex or shallow companionship. But why would he risk a deep emotional commitment—why would he risk needing her—when she constantly insists that she really does not need him?

Men are naturally promiscuous, and they will put up with "strong women" as long as the sex is good. But men are also naturally romantic. I am convinced that men have deeper feelings for their partners than women have for theirs. (Women reserve their deepest feelings for their children.) Men are therefore more emotionally vulnerable than women, and they will naturally be wary of emotionally committing to "strong women," who are far more likely to put them through emotional hell just to prove how "strong" they are. This is why "strong women" are often screwed, but infrequently wed.

It is just plain false that women can do everything a man can do, even better. Yes, there are exceptionally strong women and exceptionally weak men. But on the average, the sexes differ in countless ways. Thus it is true to say that the average man can outdo the average woman in countless pursuits, just as the average woman can outperform the average man in countless others. Furthermore, in any given couple, there are always some things the man can do better than the woman, and others the woman can do better than the man.

I have never met a man who was obsessed with ferreting out all the things that his girlfriend thought she could do better so he could prove her wrong. I know one thing: I would certainly not call him a strong man. Furthermore, I imagine that his girlfriend would quickly tire of his attempts to best her in cooking and needlework. After a time, I think she would find him downright contemptible. And when she finally walks out on him, I imagine he'll stand there in the kitchen doorway, aproned and oven-mitted, the perfect soufflé held high in triumph, and scream, "You're just afraid of strong men!"

"Strong women" are actually the most insecure, petty, and competitive women around. And these are weaknesses, not strengths.

No man wants a woman who constantly competes with him and looks for his weaknesses. Men make life competitive and insecure enough for their fellow men. So men naturally want their relationships with women to be havens from constant one-upmanship. But "strong women" won't allow that.

Another problem with "strong women" is that they tend to imitate mistaken conceptions of masculine behavior. They can imitate masculine competitiveness, but not the forms of masculine camaraderie, civility, and brotherhood that give competition some humanity. How could they, when all of these softer, communitarian virtues are associated with the femininity that "strong women" are so concerned to overcome?

"Strong women" make themselves annoying, because they inject competition where it is unwelcome. They make themselves ridiculous, because they inevitably fail in some of their attempts to outdo their men. They make themselves contemptible, because they emotionally blackmail their men into letting them win a few rounds, hoping, perhaps, that they will get this damned competitiveness out of their system.

What is a "strong woman"? A creature who has abandoned the best features of her own sex for the worst features of the other. Now that is something to fear.

January 20, 2004

THE RETURN OF EUGENICS

Late last month Helmuth Nyborg, Professor of Psychology at the University of Aarhus in Denmark, sparked an uproar in the media by calling for state measures to encourage childbearing among the intellectually gifted and discourage it among the intellectually dull. According to a report, Nyborg implored Danish politicians to "abandon the politically correct" taboo against eugenics in order to "improve the coming generations and avoid degenerates in the population."

Nyborg cited very significant differential birthrates between poorly-educated and highly-educated women. Since educated women tend to spend more time studying and working before having a family, they have fewer children on average than women with little or no formal education. Nyborg then advocated measures to reduce the workload of educated women while offering monetary incentives to the uneducated not to have children.

From a scientific standpoint, Nyborg's recommendation makes sense. The best scientific research shows a very high correlation between intelligence (as measured through IQ tests) and educational attainment, as well as a slew of other positive life outcomes. It also shows that approximately 80% of the variance in IQ scores between White individuals in industrialized countries is attributable to genetic differences.

Nyborg blames the present disrepute of eugenics on Adolf Hitler. But the fact that Hitler supported eugenics is no argument against it. Hitler enjoyed Wagner and Bruckner, and he also built *Autobahnen* and Volkswagen beetles. But that is no argument against them either. As with eugenics, we have to evaluate them on their own merits. And if we judge them to be good, then the fact that Hitler liked them is to his credit, not their discredit.

Eugenics makes sense for a very simple reason: *Intelligence is the most valuable human resource.* All progress — philosophical, artistic, scientific, technological, and political — requires high intelligence. The inventions of a Tesla or an Edison could never have been created by millions or even billions of less-gifted individuals, no matter how they cooperated, no matter what their efforts.

Yet Tesla and Edison have conferred immense benefits on the less-gifted masses, creating industries that employ millions and improving the living standards of the entire globe.

The most valuable human resource is intelligence, *and genes are the most important determinant of intelligence.* Until we discover precisely which genes influence intelligence, the only way to increase the number of highly intelligent people is for highly intelligent men to beget children with highly intelligent women. Due to the vagaries of genetics (specifically, the genetic principle of *regression toward the mean*), not all the children they produce will possess high intelligence. History shows many examples of firstborn dullards and lateborn geniuses. Thus, the highly intelligent should have large families to maximize their chances of having exceptional children. Encouraging early marriage between highly intelligent couples facilitates large families.

But modern industrial societies encourage precisely the opposite breeding pattern. Society encourages highly intelligent people to prolong their educations, leading them to delay marriage. And for many—women especially—marriage delayed is marriage denied. When such people complete their education, they often have crushing debts and must work long and irregular hours. Society also promotes selfish, materialistic lifestyles that discourage marriage and reproduction.

Furthermore, highly intelligent people are seldom intelligent enough to reject fashionable but destructive follies. Feminism denigrates marriage and reproduction and sows discord between the sexes. The fear of overpopulation encourages intelligent, responsible, public-spirited people—precisely the type of people who should have large families—to have small families or no families at all. (I accept that there are too many people in the world, but it is foolish to focus on human quantity while ignoring human quality. We need a world with fewer but better people.)

The intellectually less-gifted, however, have entirely different incentives. They leave school earlier and thus tend to marry earlier. They usually work shorter hours and have simpler, more natural tastes. They are less susceptible to feminism and other destructive notions. They therefore tend to have larger families than the highly intelligent. As for the downright stupid: they often lead lives of tax-subsidized leisure. Some welfare states actually encourage them to have large, stupid families.

Modern civilization is approaching a crisis. Progress cannot be sustained if present dysgenic trends continue. Stone Age men cannot sustain a Space Age civilization. We have to choose. If we choose continued progress, we must choose eugenics. If we continue on the present dysgenic path, then we can expect the advanced White and Asian societies to falter and then eventually collapse into tyranny, chaos, and starvation—much as African societies collapsed after the civilizing influences of the White colonial powers were withdrawn.

White societies currently stave off the consequences of their dysgenic breeding patterns by importing brains from South and East Asia. But this is no solution. Aside from the racially, culturally, and politically destructive effects of non-White immigration, this policy is not globally sustainable. While we are importing Asian brains, they are importing our dysgenic culture. Once the dysgenic regime is global, importing brains will be impossible, and collapse will be inevitable.

A eugenics program requires neither tyrannical enforcement nor mandatory participation. All it requires are the proper incentives. For highly intelligent men, we could write off a year's worth of student loans for every child they father. For highly intelligent women, we could offer a free year of higher education for every child they bear—but to encourage early marriage and reproduction, the free education would be available only *after* they have children. Tax incentives could encourage the highly intelligent to have large families and the less-gifted to have smaller ones. As for the downright stupid: they could easily be persuaded to undergo sterilization. A flashy new car could remove them from the gene pool forever.

Professor Nyborg is probably not the last advocate of eugenics, but the first of their return. If only one nation adopts eugenics, the others will be compelled to follow—simply out of fear. For if one nation adopts eugenics while the rest continue down the present path, that nation—even tiny Denmark—will end up ruling the world.

October 9, 2003

Race-Mixing vs. Diversity

There is a great deal of propaganda today favoring race-mixing or miscegenation. So I thought it useful to set down some of the reasons I oppose it.

First and foremost, I oppose miscegenation because it destroys every race that practices it.

A race is a biological subspecies, an extended family. Distinct races probably came about as follows. First, a subgroup was isolated from the rest of the species. Second, the isolated group was differentiated from the rest of the species.

There are two main factors that give rise to the differences between races. First is what can simply be described as the "playfulness" of nature, by which I mean nature's apparent innate tendency toward the creation of diverse new forms, either by producing new genetic "code" or through novel combinations of the same genetic material. Second are the selective pressures of unique environmental conditions, which cull some of nature's innovations, encourage others, and probably remain indifferent to most.

Subjected to these differentiating factors for sufficient time, an isolated subgroup will acquire new and distinct characteristics. These characteristics will eventually be spread homogenously throughout the group as long as there are no barriers to breeding within the group. (If the isolated population is split into several genetically exclusive communities, these communities will have distinct genetic identities, and the population as a whole will not have a homogenous genetic identity.)

The new race's unique genetic identity will be maintained only as long as it remains genetically separate and exclusive, breeding within itself and not breeding with other races. Miscegenation undoes this. Thus it destroys millennia of racial evolution.

For years now, the leading voices of our cultural establishment have been telling us that diversity is an unconditional good. You'd think we could never have too much diversity. This, of course, is nonsense. Racial and ethnic diversity always weaken any group's ability to harmoniously promote individual and collective goals.

And even where diversity is good, it is not unconditionally good. You can have too much of it. Variety may be the spice of life, for instance, but if one cooks a new dish every night one will never attain the excellence that comes only from repeated practice.

It is ironic that miscegenation is promoted by the very people who make a cult of diversity, because in the long run *miscegenation completely destroys racial diversity.* In the short run, of course, miscegenation does increase diversity by filling the world with a colorful array of mongrels. But in the long run, as pure racial types disappear and mongrels mix with mongrels, this diversity will give way to a brown uniformity. Thus the only way to maintain racial diversity over the long term is to avoid miscegenation.

Miscegenation is sometimes promoted because people recognize, however dimly, that racially diverse societies are unworkable. But if racially homogenous societies are the most workable, then why not preserve and improve upon the many existing racially homogenous societies? Why not divide up multiracial societies into a number of racially homogenous ones?

Surely this racial nationalist approach is a much more realistic and workable solution than the "utopia" (in reality a dystopia) proposed by the "miscegenationalists": A single global state ruling a single homogenous mongrel population, a global state that will emerge only after countless wars and untold bloodshed, and a mongrel population that will emerge only after generations of racial and ethnic conflict (and the forcible extermination of populations that refuse to blend).

The same argument applies to another ideal of the diversity-mongers: multiculturalism. The multiculturalists do not advocate a plurality of distinct culturally homogeneous states. That would be ethnic nationalism. Instead, multiculturalists advocate multiple cultures *within each state.* This is why multiculturalists favor unlimited immigration. How else would the Icelanders be enriched by the presence of Bantu and Hmong and Papuans?

But when different cultures are forced to live and work together, the differences between them are bound to cause conflict. If the differences are sharp enough, a society will become Balkanized, torn apart by ethnic hatred and wars of secession. To avoid conflict, cultures have to minimize their differences. Thus the pursuit of social harmony in multicultural societies leads eventually to cultural uniformity, to the destruction of real cultural diversity. This is the famous American "melting pot."

But whether it is by Balkanization or assimilation, multiculturalism destroys every culture that practices it. Thus the only way to preserve both harmony and cultural diversity is to have a plurality of ethnically homogenous states. Cultural diversity, like racial diversity, requires separation.

Our enemies have spent a great deal of time, money, and energy promoting the appreciation of diversity. Let's seize the profits of their investment by showing that miscegenation and multiculturalism destroy diversity and that we racial and cultural nationalists are the only ones who truly respect and preserve it.

April 6, 2005

MIKE VS. EMORY

Emory University declared the 2000–2001 school year to be the "Year of Reconciliation" for important issues affecting the University, and I naïvely took this claim at face value. According to the Year of Reconciliation website,

> our aim was to celebrate the turn of the millennium through exploring a theme that highlighted the work of our faculty and students, promoted interdisciplinary dialogue about matters of importance to us all, encouraged discussion of the future of our university, and provided opportunities to use our thinking and discussion as first steps to action. We chose a theme that would be broad enough so that each member of the community could interpret it in a way meaningful to herself or himself.

I decided to interpret the Year of Reconciliation in a meaningful way. I raised a controversial, very important issue which I didn't believe academia (or the general public, for that matter) has fully considered: the possibility that observed differences in both scholastic achievement and in violent crime between whites and blacks result partly from genetic differences between the races. I knew, of course, that the issue has always been a very controversial one. Nonetheless, I thought that at a university, ostensibly the highest citadel of rational thought, during a supposed "Year of Reconciliation," the arguments for both sides of this unresolved issue could be subjected to critical analysis, leading to more enlightened conclusions on the matter, or so I'd hoped.

I broached the subject in an October 6, 2000 editorial for the school newspaper, the *Emory Wheel*, in which I discussed UC-Berkeley Professor Emeritus of Psychology Arthur Jensen's most recent (1998) book on the subject of intelligence, *The g Factor*. In this book Jensen, among (many) other things, provides empirical evidence suggesting that Blacks and Whites differ in "g" (general intelligence), and he hypothesizes that this difference stems from genetic differences between the races. I soon learned that Arthur Jensen has held this opinion since 1969, that he has published over 400 articles in various peer-reviewed scientific journals, and that he was (and is) well-respected by his colleagues in the field, both as a rigorous scientist and as a man of impeccable personal integrity. This opinion is shared even by those who strongly disagree with his stance on race differences in g, an area that comprises only a small portion of his contributions to the scientific study of intelligence.

I raised the possibility of inherent racial difference with regard to the wisdom of continuing compensatory programs (like Affirmative Action and Head Start) designed to get Blacks on an equal footing with Whites. I reasoned that if Jensen's hypothesis were correct these programs could never succeed, and could only do harm in the long run by misappropriating resources better spent elsewhere. Thus, a critical examination of Jensen's most recent work in the area should certainly have been in order during the Year of Reconciliation.

EMORY'S RESPONSE

In the next issue of the school newspaper, an open letter to me from then University President William Chace appeared. Besides questioning my motivation for writing the editorial (something I had expected), he made the patently false claim that "the jury is not out on Jensen," meaning that his hypothesis had been discarded as untenable. Prior to writing my editorial, I had made *absolutely certain* that Jensen's hypothesis was not only being actively debated, but was also steadily winning the support of experts in his field. I found that earlier that very same year (2000) Jensen was defending his book on the publicly-accessible *Psycoloquy*, "a refereed international, interdisciplinary electronic journal sponsored by the American Psychological Association (APA) and indexed by APA's PsycINFO and the Institute for Scientific Information." I smiled, thinking to myself how embarrassed Chace would be when he had to eat his own words, for surely at least one Emory faculty member up to speed on the subject would realize that Jensen's work was *by no means* scientifically disproven. Did Chace really think I was stupid enough to defend such a controversial position were it not justifiable by current research in the field?

Chace also decried as "wholly repugnant" my suggestion that compensatory programs should be reconsidered if they could not achieve their stated goals. According to him, Affirmative Action and Head Start are justified because they punish Whites, regardless of whether or not they help Blacks. He concluded his letter by "demanding" that the Emory community respond to me, using "all of the instruments of reason and civil discourse — and no other means."

My reaction at that point was one of furtive amusement. I was certain that at least one individual in the Emory community would expose Chace's mistake in dismissing Jensen in such a curt, summary fashion. I wrote Chace an open letter in return, a modified edition of which appeared in the next issue of the school newspaper (apparently the newspaper made an exception for Chace on its policy of not allowing directly addressed open letters: I was told I wasn't permitted to address Chace directly).

I received countless emails concerning my article from students for about the next month, and found out that my article had been the subject of discussion in several classes. I also was contacted by the president of a student group called RACES (Racial and Cultural Education Source). He told me that his group was going to schedule a forum the coming Wednesday to discuss the issue. I told him that I thought a forum was a great idea, but that Wednesday would be a bad time because I had a biology test to take that evening, and I didn't like the idea of having to take the test and defend my column in front of a potentially hostile crowd all in the same evening.

His response, as quoted from an email I received that weekend, was:

> I do not think that I was clear on the subject matter of the forum on Wednesday. We will not take a large time to discuss your editorial — we are more concerned with the reconciliation of the matter at hand and how we as an Emory community can learn to educate each other about racial differences and learn how to be together here as a commu-

nity. Your concerns are valid about walking into a potentially hostile environment, but I think that many people will agree with me that you have done that to yourself in your editorial . . . many people have expressed to me that they felt it important you attend. However, if you cannot attend the forum will go on. This issue needs to be addressed and the community needs to voice their opinions and we need to continue forward in a constructive manner toward bringing all cultures together on campus. This matter is much bigger than a single person.

I was astounded that this individual thought that the matter could be adequately resolved if no one were present to defend Jensen's position. I had two problems with his reasoning. First, I strongly disagreed with his priorities: Bringing people together is great, but not if it comes at the expense of the truth. The latter should always have priority. But questions of truth, apparently, played no role in his thinking. Second, even if "bringing cultures together" were more important than truth, one could never hope to bring people together on anything but the most superficial level if the issues keeping different groups apart are not permitted to be discussed in a forthright manner.

From his email I got the impression that I was going to walk into a kangaroo court, a show trial where I would be presented as the obviously wrong racist, a farce where the verdict had already been decided and nothing I said would make any difference. Why else would only a short time be devoted to my editorial? Why else would the forum be able to continue if I didn't attend? Only if the judgment were already determined in advance would these things not make a difference.

The forum proved to be the travesty I'd envisioned.[1] As a news article in the *Wheel* points out, I had to go up against a tag team of six professors, all of whom argued against Jensen. (Interestingly, none of them had expertise in psychology.) Combined, they had 30 minutes to present their case, while I only had five.

---

[1] For local news coverage of the event, see http://www.countercurrents.com/2010/08/polignano-video/

Needless to say, five minutes were insufficient time to make a case even if I were an excellent public speaker and possessed the knowledge of Jensen himself. I did my best to address each of the points raised by the six professors, but since they gave me only 50 seconds per professor it was an impossible task that I was foolish even to attempt. I also got the impression that nothing I said really mattered: most audience members certainly didn't come with open minds; they came to pronounce judgment.

It was evident from their remarks that none of the professors had bothered to read what Jensen had to say about race. Nowhere did he argue that races were fixed, discrete categories, as the professors claimed. Rather, Jensen defines them as "breeding populations that, as a result of natural selection, have come to differ statistically in the relative frequencies of many polymorphic genes" (*The* g *Factor*, p. 418).

I pointed out that Jensen made use of Stanford geneticist Luigi Luca Cavalli-Sforza's comprehensive study of population differences in allele frequencies, published in 1994 as *The History and Geography of Human Genes*. ("Alleles" are alternative forms of a gene.) The main analysis in this book is based on blood and tissue specimens obtained from representative samples of 42 populations, from every continent and the Pacific Islands. All the individuals in these samples were aboriginal or indigenous to the areas in which they were selected; their ancestors have lived in the same geographic area since at least 1492, a familiar date selected to mark the beginning of extensive European explorations and consequent major population movements. Measuring the allele frequencies of 120 alleles for 49 different genes, Cavalli-Sforza and his co-workers then calculated the genetic distance between each group and every other group, and constructed a *genetic linkage tree* based on this data. The entire tree and a simplified version containing larger groupings appear on the opposite page.

I explained that whether one uses the term "race" or "population" to describe the groups Cavalli-Sforza researches is merely a matter of sematics. I also noted that the number of human racial groups is arbitrary, varying based on how specific one wants to get on the genetic linkage tree. While racial categorizations such as "White," "Black," and "Asian" are social constructs, they correlate to a large extent with the biological groupings as shown on the genetic linkage tree. "Whites," for instance, all share ancestry in the "Caucasoid" category. "Black" is the social category containing the greatest genetic variance: Although a New Guinean

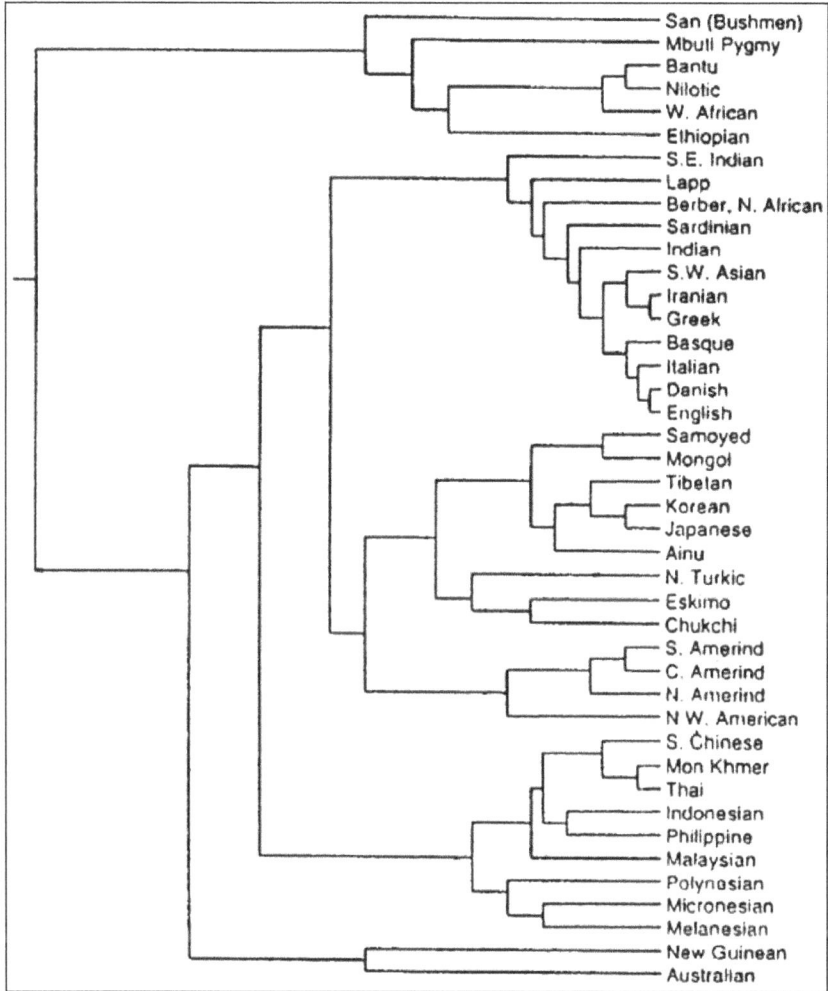

and a Bushman are just as genetically distant from one another as an Englishman and a Bushman, New Guineans and Bushmen both evolved far closer to the equator (hence facing similar selective pressures during the past 100,000 years or so of human evolution) than Englishmen, whose ancestors had to endure the selective pressure of an Ice Age. Hence, for traits under selective pressure like skin color, cranial shape and capacity, and mental ability, New Guineans and Bushmen resemble one another and thus would be socially categorized as "Black."

However, no one besides myself at the forum was willing to acknowledge *any* biological influence on socially-identified racial groups. After anthropology professor George Armelagos said that "race is not a useful biological construct," I asked how it was that forensic anthropologists could reliably and correctly identify the race of a human skull if race had no correlation with biology. I also pointed out that races differ in frequencies of certain diseases, and that mainstream science has found that some of these differences have genetic components. For instance, I pointed out a study showing that some people of European ancestry possess a gene providing resistance to HIV infection, believed to have arisen in the population because it also provides resistance to the bubonic plague which swept through Europe in the Middle Ages. But these rebuttals fell on deaf ears. The prevailing idea put forth at the forum was that racial classification was "bad science," in addition to being inherently evil and "hateful," and no one besides myself challenged that idea.

In the weeks following the forum, I met with a number of Emory professors who were willing to admit privately that Jensen's findings might be correct. But to their shame and my disgust none of the scientists was willing to do so publicly. Out of apathy or fear they were willing to let stand Chace's false assertion that "the jury is not out on Jensen." The one professor who was willing to defend me publicly was James Gouinlock, a professor of philosophy who was far better informed about Jensen's work than the scientists who attacked it. Gouinlock wrote a letter to the editor of the *Wheel* defending me. But the *Wheel* refused to print it, or even acknowledge its receipt. I also learned that most White students at Emory were convinced from personal experience that race and IQ are linked. But only two students were willing to defend me publicly, one on scientific grounds, the other on First Amendment grounds. An Emory alumnus, John R. Morgan, M.D., also wrote a letter to the *Wheel* in my defense.

I created a discussion group on LearnLink, Emory's internal

computer network, to examine the issue further. I was interested in hearing if anybody had any substantive criticism of Jensen's work, since the professors at the forum entirely misrepresented Jensen's position on key issues like race. The responses I received were mostly *ad hominem* attacks with ridiculous or irrelevant disparaging comments, although some productive discussion did take place.

I came to realize that an extremely nasty and highly motivated minority of faculty and students held the campus in the grip of fear. The purpose of my public humiliation was clear: It was a warning. Anyone who publicly acknowledged scientific facts or personal experiences about the reality of race could expect the same treatment.

Arthur Jensen is the Galileo of our times. And to its eternal shame, Emory University refused to look into the telescope.

THE RECONCILIATION SYMPOSIUM

As could be predicted by Emory's response to Jensen's work, the following Spring's Reconciliation Symposium proved to be a one-sided farce (a left-sided farce) which reconciled absolutely nothing. The symposiasts were a racially and sexually diverse bunch who held blandly homogenous, predictably "progressive" opinions about everything. No reconciliation was needed, because contradictory data and contrary viewpoints were never discussed. A list of some of the headlines from the *Wheel*'s Reconciliation Symposium coverage speaks volumes:

- "Gender balance tipped in men's favor, Epps says"
- "Social relief for oppressed minorities dominates social justice discussion"
- "Cole exhorts audience to mix color lines in race reconciliation panel discussion"
- "Reconciliation crumbles *sans* democracy, prof says"
- "Emory prof says restorative justice more effective than death penalty"
- "Chopp exhorts students to look at world from global perspective, not myopic one"

Fortunately, some students protested. Indeed, three of the six editorials written about the Symposium deal with this topic.

The best of these is the staff editorial, which rightly chided the symposium as "a fantasy reconciliation" and noted "it takes a great stretch of the imagination to consider an academic summit with an almost complete monopoly of opinion in nearly every field to be a productive advancement of debate."

Another editorial suggests a "mini-symposium" directed at students, with one of the panels entitled "Reconciling the Opposing Sides in the Race and Intelligence Debate." The author notes, "When controversy flared over this issue in the fall, professors and administrators moved quickly to squelch debate on one side. This gives the impression that only a few students believe that race and intelligence are connected. Casual conversations tell a different story."

The final column, entitled "Reconciliation Requires Vigorous Debate," dealt with the panel "Reconciling Race, Ethnicity and Other Lines that Divide Us." After noting that "there was not any reconciliation going on in this discussion because no one offered a strong dissent to any of the panelists," he writes, "For all the senseless and malicious dribble *Wheel* columnist Michael Polignano spewed last fall, he had a point in suggesting that the academy lacks a spectrum of academic thought."

Over the past few years, I have researched the work of Jensen and others regarding race differences. Contrary to popular belief, I've found that the preponderance of scientific evidence supports the view that genetics play just as much (and likely more) of a role than environment as far as racial differences in mental ability are concerned.

AN AMUSING POSTSCRIPT

Later on that year, my picture appeared on the cover of Emory's 2001–2002 course catalog. A black student, trying to shame Emory into catering even more slavishly to ever-disgruntled minorities, complained that the picture was somehow an endorsement of my ideas. But that is preposterous. Emory only wanted me for my body, not for my mind.

October 6, 2003

Course Catalog
EMORY COLLEGE 2001–2002

EMORY NEEDS TO CHOOSE:
UNITY OR DIVERSITY

As this school year begins, I cannot help but think of the divisive issues with which we all had to deal toward the end of the spring semester. In particular, the relatively extreme measures proposed for dealing with race relations on the Emory campus come to mind: the founding of an organization dedicated to "fighting racism and promoting unity" whenever and wherever it can, talk of the addition of yet another politically correct class to the lineup of politically correct classes already included as part of the College's distribution requirements, the banishment of a fraternity from campus for daring to display a flag they view as a sign of their heritage but others find "offensive," and so on.

Although the severity of the proposed actions would lead one to think otherwise, after hearing the opinions of several students, I've found that with the exception of a few who have very strong opinions one way or the other, most students seem quite indifferent about the issue of race relations on campus. Most are willing to accept the *status quo:* no overt racism, yet also no "unity" in the sense of support for dismantling the racial/ethnic cliques that exist on campus. For this reason I'm hesitant to support any organization that views these cliques as evidence of "racism" and has their elimination as one of its long-term goals.

While it's true that allowing these cliques to continue will perpetuate some level of "polarization" on campus, one has to acknowledge the fact that a true belief in multiculturalism involves respecting cultural boundaries, and not attempting to push all the varying groups into one cohesive whole. A lack of "unity" is the trade-off Emory must accept as long as it chooses to regard all groups as equal and doesn't actively promote a dominant "culture" on campus. We all must acknowledge that "being tolerant" of those of a different race, ideological background, or sexual orientation means allowing groups that accentuate or even celebrate these differences to exist. In short, we must accept that "diversity" and "unity" share an inverse relationship.

Wanting to associate closely with others who share a lot in common with oneself is entirely normal. It's as natural for those of minority racial/ethnic groups to want to associate with one another as it is natural for conservative thinkers to want to associate with other conservatives, homosexuals to want to associate with other homosexuals, and Catholics to want to meet with and associate with other Catholics. While this doesn't mean students should close their minds to those who differ from them in terms of ideology, sexual orientation, race, religion, and so on, the best goal for which any student organization should aim is mutual respect between the various groups on campus, not to push groups together that cherish their unique identity and wish to remain separate.

In short, I don't wish for the intolerance certain groups and individuals have shown toward the Kappa Alpha Order to extend towards other groups. We must all learn to get along in order to function in the real world. However, trying to push students to accept "unity" at the expense of preserving cultural distinctions is quite unwise and could potentially lead to a backlash.

Also at stake is Emory's goal of preserving academic freedom: How would a "unified" campus, for example, deal with someone who believes that homosexuality is morally and biologically wrong, or someone who believes that racial differences in intelligence and behavior are partly due to genes? Although such opinions might be enormously unpopular and would likely lead to tensions between groups on campus, a truly "tolerant" campus would welcome the open discussion of these opinions. What about a "unified" campus: Would these ideas be judged on the merits the arguments that could be presented in their defense, or would they be summarily dismissed as "homophobic" or "racist"? Let us keep these issues in mind as we enter this "Year of Reconciliation," lest we fall into the trap of narrow-mindedness and strict uniformity of thought enforced on a campus-wide scale.

September 5, 2000

GENES MAY DETERMINE RACIAL ATTRIBUTES

Before I get started, I want to say that honesty and open discussion are mandatory for making any sort of headway in racial reconciliation. What I'm about to say will almost certainly generate controversy and will undoubtedly offend some people, but it needs to be said in order for any sort of real progress to be made.

Unfortunately, it's sometimes necessary to reopen old wounds so that healing can occur properly. If I believed that one should sacrifice things like truth and honesty for the sake of being popular and "politically correct," I'd be studying for a career in politics instead of in science.

That said, I think that the road to racial understanding should begin with a look at some common stereotypes that exist regarding racial differences and see what, if any, truth exists behind them. By far, the deepest fissure that exists in the US is between Whites and Blacks. Some common stereotypes about Blacks by Whites are that Blacks are, in general, more prone to crime, more violent, and less intelligent than Whites. Obviously, if these stereotypes aren't true, then all of us have a moral obligation to speak out whenever we hear these stereotypes voiced, and should work hard to eliminate them entirely. For example, if Blacks and Whites commit crime at equal rates, then we should outlaw racial profiling not just because it's unfair, but also because it wouldn't help reduce crime.

Unfortunately, as much as some of us would want to believe otherwise, each and every one of the above stereotypes has some truth to it. A well-researched study released just last year has found that Blacks are 50 times more likely to commit a violent crime against a White than Whites are to commit a violent crime against Blacks. You can review the data yourself at www.amren.com/colrcrim.html.

As far as intelligence is concerned, Dr. Arthur Jensen, Professor Emeritus of Educational Psychology at the University of California-Berkeley, has devoted much of his 40 year tenure at Berkeley to the study of general intelligence, or g. His work has made him one of the most frequently cited figures in contemporary psychology. Jensen believes that g is up to 80% heritable in adults, meaning that variations in intelligence between adults are due 80% to genes and 20% to environment, within human populations, i.e.: within "races."

In his book *The g Factor*, Jensen also deals with the differences in g that exist between human racial populations. General intelligence correlates highly with creativity, socioeconomic status, educational attainment, and a slew of other variables. As far as Whites and Blacks are concerned, he notes that the mean black IQ is 15 points lower than the mean white IQ, even after taking extensive measures to eliminate test bias. In the book, he proposes a theory, which he calls "the default hypothesis," which holds that "the proximal causes of both individual differences and population differences in heritable psychological traits are essentially the same, and are continuous variables."

A questionnaire survey presented elsewhere in the book shows that Jensen is not alone in his beliefs. Of 661 experts in the fields of differential psychology, psychometrics, and behavioral genetics, 45% were of the opinion that the Black-White difference in IQ "is a product of both genetic and environmental variation," and only 15% felt that the difference is due to environment alone. So, it is indeed possible that truth exists behind the "racist" claim that Blacks are inherently less intelligent. How do we deal with this possibility?

Not through censorship.

Dr. Jensen's work is a prime example of how political correctness can endanger academic freedom. In the past, left-wing radicals physically assaulted him during one of his talks at the University of Minnesota, and the university did nothing to punish the assailants. I wonder what would happen if he came to Emory? Would he be arrested by the Emory Police Department for committing a so-called "act of intolerance" if he were to give a talk in which he mentioned that class and race differences in intelligence were primarily the result of genetic differences?

What we need here is open discussion. Like all scientific

work, Dr. Jensen's theories are subject to refutation through empirical evidence. So far, I've read plenty of attacks on Jensen's motives, but I have yet to find any scientific articles that show any major flaws in his data or his conclusions. So, I guess I'd have to agree with him and say that genes (and not racism, past inequalities, or anything else) are primarily responsible for Blacks' lower status on the socioeconomic ladder in the US.

Should I, or anyone else, feel somehow guilty for even daring to consider the possibility that races differ by more than just skin color? Should scientists not perform research that might threaten commonly held beliefs about race? Are the social pressures forbidding the open discussion of "racist" ideas the same type of social pressures Galileo faced for daring to question the belief that the earth is the center of the solar system, or Darwin for daring to question the Bible's version of creation? Why was I always told in school and through the media growing up that all races are inherently equal in intelligence, when in actuality the debate still rages on within scientific circles?

I'm not saying Jensen's explanation is necessarily right, just that alternative explanations are possibly wrong, and that we'll never know for sure until his theories can be openly discussed and debated and more research is done. It's people like those who attacked Dr. Jensen who are the true close-minded ones. They can't comprehend that if he is right, then it does us no good to pretend that compensatory programs like Affirmative Action and Head Start will eventually put Blacks on an equal footing with Whites. On the other hand, if he's wrong, then we have a responsibility to help Blacks achieve their potential, and rid the world of racism. But we need open discussion before any of this can happen.

October 6, 2000

AN OPEN RESPONSE TO PRESIDENT CHACE

In retrospect, I see that the wording I employed in my article of last week was a bit too provocative, confrontational, and subject to misinterpretation. For one, I did not choose the headline "Genes May Determine Racial Attributes." In fact, the first time I saw that headline was when I picked up a copy of Friday's *Wheel*. Second, I shouldn't have taken such clear sides with Jensen, especially since I didn't have the space to present an opposing viewpoint. Third, I provided a link to a study funded by an organization of dubious background. Although this doesn't affect the validity of the underlying facts, I can understand how referring to a controversial study could be misconstrued as an endorsement of the organization that sponsored the study. I intended for the article to raise issues that require open discussion and rational debate, and I hoped that the controversy generated would expedite this process. Yet my one-sided approach alienated many, which I regret.

While I regret that many members of the Emory community took extreme offense at my words, I'm not sorry I wrote the article. For I know that my intentions were noble and were based in an unbiased search for truth and understanding, not the belittlement of any particular group. I wouldn't have mentioned Jensen if I didn't think his work had merit to it, although I admit that Jensen might be wrong. If I am in error, any apology I might make for these beliefs in the future will note that this error was not caused by ignorance or bigotry, but rather by honest mistake.

That said, I realize that Arthur Jensen is but one of many thinkers who have dealt with the "color line." I apologize for the lack of clarity, but when I wrote, "I have yet to find major flaws in his data or his conclusions," I more specifically meant that I have yet to find any criticism that substantively rules out Jensen's default hypothesis. In fact, Jensen still defends his work before scientific commentators on the American Psychological Association's Web site *Psycoloquy* (www.cogsci.soton.ac.uk/cgi/psyc/newpsy).

I merely wish to stress the need not to suppress research into the subject and for people to realize that Jensen's hypothesis is potentially correct. I have the feeling that right now, many would immediately discard it as "racist" or "ignorant," as I'm sure is currently done in many anthropology and sociology courses at Emory. If his hypothesis is correct, then we need to consider a genetic solution to narrowing the IQ gap between self-defined "Whites" and self-defined "Blacks." Such a solution need not violate anyone's rights. I'm of the firm belief that human problems are best solved by increasing human knowledge, and that in the long-run increased knowledge leads to greater human happiness, not the opposite. Suppression of scientific inquiry on ideological grounds constitutes one of the worst forms of thought control, and is anathema to a free society.

Trust me, if I had been writing a book on the subject instead of an op-ed piece, I would have certainly examined other researchers' hypotheses instead of aligning myself with Jensen. My article wasn't meant as a critical analysis of the varying intelligence theories. I merely wanted to give a specific example of suppression that has occurred to a particular researcher, whose work is by no means "discredited."

Growing up, I was only given a one-sided perspective on the issue: that all races are inherently equal in intelligence and innate behavioral characteristics. Any doubts I had I kept to myself, thinking that once I attained the next higher educational level I'd learn exactly why I was wrong. Once I looked into the issue on my own and saw some of the suppressive tactics used by radical student organizations and college administrators against politically incorrect professors, I had to ask, "Why?" If what these people thought was so obviously "wrong," then why did brute-force tactics have to be used to silence them?

Then I realized I was naïve in thinking that complete academic freedom is a goal towards which all modern universities strive. It isn't.

Let's face it, if an assistant professor at Emory had come to Wednesday's Race and Cultural Education Source forum and supported Jensen's position on the race/IQ issue, he could kiss his chances of ever achieving tenure goodbye regardless of the evidence he presented. I can't even begin to speculate as to the political pressures University administrators need to conform in order to maintain both a school's funding and its reputation, but I do know that the left-wing influence on certain fields, including cultural anthropology, sociology, and political science, is well-documented. Any theory questioning equality, especially human genetic equality, faces summary dismissal on ideological, not scientific grounds. The empirical standards required by the "hard" sciences reduce the appeal of these disciplines to political ideologues, but some exist and they do make their presence known.

Here's but one example: Despite his contributions to the field of evolutionary biology (which I readily acknowledge), Stephen Jay Gould is a self-avowed Marxist. His ideological bias towards a world of impossible economic equality prohibits him from even considering a theory that questions whether genetic equality exists between human groups. Not surprisingly, he has been one of Jensen's most ardent critics.

I've also seen cases of outrageous media bias in reporting politically incorrect stories, particularly those that involve race. One example is the outrageous libel the *Atlanta Constitution* printed after an interview with Nobel Laureate William Shockley in 1981. Shockley, who co-invented the transistor in 1948 and was a awarded the Medal of Merit (America's highest civilian honor) by US President Harry S. Truman for heading America's anti-submarine warfare research during World War II, was compared to Adolf Hitler for merely revealing his highly detailed research and findings regarding race, IQ, and dysgenic trends. His mathematical analyses were curtly dismissed as "rubbish," and he was portrayed as an ignorant racist throughout the article.

Shockley sued the paper for $1.25 million for grossly distorting and misrepresenting his position. The trial, held before a mixed-race jury, ultimately ruled in his favor, but only awarded him $1 compensation (and no costs) for a trial which cost him about $80,000. Such was the slap in the face given to one of the twentieth century's greatest scientists for simply defending his politically incorrect findings.

Now, I'm finding myself vilified for suggesting that the work of such scholars as William Shockley, Arthur Jensen, J. Philippe Rushton, Richard Herrnstein, Hans Eysenck, Michael Levin, and Glayde Whitney (to name a few) might actually have scientific merit. Apparently, I'm not allowed to think that. I'm not supposed to question certain ideas. Why else would I be made to feel so unwelcome here on Emory's supposedly "tolerant" campus?

George Orwell once wrote, "In a time of universal deceit, telling the truth is a revolutionary act." I feel I've been deceived, and I'm telling the truth.

October 13, 2000

THE RACIAL INTELLIGENCE GAP IS STILL AN UNRESOLVED ISSUE

A lot of people probably view me as the antagonist in the story of the recent racial debate at Emory, but discussion of the sort we had October 11 is exactly what we need in order to make progress. I think I can safely say that nearly everyone, myself included, left the Winship Ballroom that evening feeling better than upon entering. Since then, I haven't received any additional hate mail from Emory students, and I've even made amends with a few people who sent me such mail.

I hope everyone understands that the Band-Aid solution of not talking about race and IQ in order to not offend others simply won't do. Nor will adding a "cultural sensitivity" class to the required academic curriculum. I don't take pleasure in bringing up this controversial issue, and I'd avoid it if I could, but if we don't discuss the IQ gap and its possible causes soon, the country will suffer in the long run.

If the cause of the IQ gap is partially genetic, then well-intentioned programs like Affirmative Action won't succeed and will only lead to more problems in the long run. Whites who get overlooked in favor of minorities will acquire unspoken resentment, and minorities will never know for sure if they've gotten a job for their skills or their race. When our country enters its next period of economic hardship, which it undoubtedly will eventually, unspoken resentment could easily turn into overt hatred. Only if we discuss these issues now, while rational debate and discourse is still an option, can we hope to avoid this unpleasantness and the threat it poses to the country.

Believe it or not, I've received a lot of support since my October 6 column appeared. Unfortunately none of these students voiced their opinions at the Racial and Cultural Education Source forum held in response to that column, which tells me we still have quite some way to go before we have completely open discourse on the subject. Ironically, on a day—National Coming Out Day—when many students were coming out of the closet by being honest with the world about their sexual orientation, no other students came out of the closet with respect to their true opinions on my column.

Such a response might lead student groups like RACES and the Black Student Alliance to come to the erroneous conclusion that I'm the only one on campus who thinks that genetics might play some role in shaping behavioral differences between races, or that discussing this possibility is worthwhile. If they make this mistake, they are only fooling themselves. To use the words of Anthropology Professor Ben Freed at last week's RACES forum, I am not "an individual flaw in the system."

I'll therefore continue speaking not only for myself, but also for those individuals who have chosen not to speak. As word of the events that have taken place here continue to spread past Emory's campus, I'm hoping the "system" will soon come under close scrutiny by independent observers.

After all, since all of the scientific criticisms I've heard so far are addressed at some length in *The g Factor* itself, I'm led to believe that many of the faculty members who criticized me for supposedly not doing enough research should have followed their own advice before commenting. As I stated in my original column, no criticisms I read so far "refute" Arthur Jensen's work.

By giving students the false impression that Jensen's work has been discredited, the "system" has committed an act of gross intellectual dishonesty. Disagreeing with Jensen's work is one thing, but abusing a position of authority by saying it has been "refuted" and cannot possibly be true is quite another. I therefore call upon Freed and all the other faculty members who have directly stated or indirectly implied that Jensen's work has been "refuted" to take responsibility for their statements and issue an apology to both the Emory community and to Jensen.

I also ask anyone who believes that race has no biological basis to consider the fact that only 30 years ago, many scientists said the same thing about gender. The differences between men and women were thought to be purely physical in nature, and any behavioral differences that existed were believed to be purely environmental. Anyone who said otherwise was dubbed a "sexist," and sexists were automatically guilty of a conspiracy against women to keep them oppressed. Radical feminists enforced this line of thought, and actively sought to acquire all the benefits of being a man, while eschewing the responsibilities.

Fortunately, most mainstream feminists today are readily willing to admit that men and women do differ behaviorally as well as physically as a result of genetic differences between the sexes. Nearly all psychologists hold this view, which is taught in Emory's introductory psychology classes. Most people understand that it's not disrespectful to women in any way to acknowledge that men and women are complementary, not identical, not just in the physical sense but also in a behavioral sense, and that the two are intimately related. The behavioral reason that men fight over women, and not vice versa, relates back to the physical reason that sperm "fight" to get the ovum, and not vice versa.

Although sociologists might believe that gender, which evolved over hundreds of millions of years, is headed for extinction because of the societal changes that have occurred during the last 40 years, real scientists can see the flaws in this reasoning. Humanity will disappear before sex disappears, and that's certainly not a bad thing.

And while the different races of *Homo sapiens* that evolved over the past 110,000 years could theoretically disappear if interbreeding occurred on a massive scale, humans overwhelmingly tend to marry within their own race, so they're not going to go away anytime soon either. Just as with sexual differences, we need to acknowledge the innate group differences that exist rather than attempt to fool ourselves into believing they don't exist.

November 3, 2000

POLITICAL CORRECTNESS DOESN'T BRING RECONCILIATION

Unfortunately, the racial aspects of much of what I wrote and spoke about last semester overshadowed a larger problem I had hoped to address: political correctness and how it can infringe upon intellectual diversity.

I don't mind what people's opinions are on my assertion that race and IQ may be correlated, or the implications that they have on race relations, as long as everyone voicing an opinion can defend his or her position with rational arguments. Last semester, when I saw that continuing to argue my position was becoming an exercise in futility, I simply stopped doing so. I didn't stop because I had changed my mind or because I thought the University had come anywhere close to giving students equal exposure to all sides of the issue, but rather because I deemed it pointless, even with the silent supporters I had, to continue arguing.

I expected disagreement, but I thought that everyone who disagreed would have good reasons for doing so, and that each would deal logically with the arguments I threw back. I also expected those who disagreed to reach a consensus as to why they disagreed, believing that in the process of reconciling all sides of the debate consistent "pro" arguments and consistent "con" arguments would emerge. I quickly learned that, as much as universities envision themselves as bastions of academic freedom where ideas can stand or fall on their own merits, the rebuttals I made were met with silence or non sequiturs.

Furthermore, it seemed that in the scramble to find arguments opposing me, any conceivable argument would do, regardless of whether the arguments contradicted each other. Some said race didn't exist, some said it did. Some said IQ doesn't measure anything, others said it did. Some said the IQ gap is real but is due to biased testing, others said biased tests weren't a legitimate explanation. Some professors said the research I cited must be wrong, others, behind closed doors, said it is potentially correct but that it is irresponsible to draw conclusions from it because of methodological flaws. Did it escape people's attention that the psychologists and anthropologists at this school have some apparent reconciling to do themselves? I'm hoping that even those who disagree with the stance I took last semester can at least see some of the contradictions in the arguments used to oppose me, and wish to see them resolved as much as I do.

Along the way, several individuals wrongly suggested I was attempting to legitimize racism, and that my mind had been made up from the start. Such *ad hominem* attacks only got worse the longer I stood my ground, so in the end I decided it was taking too much time and energy and simply withdrew from the debate.

This semester, I can't help but smile and think, "I told you so," each time I look in the *Wheel* and read the editorials relating to reconciliation and race relations. The consensus, even shared by those who despised my column that suggested a connection between race and IQ last semester, is that there is no reconciliation happening during this Year of Reconciliation because only one viewpoint is ever expressed: the politically correct one. A *Wheel* staff editorial ("Not much debate," January 30) rightly criticized the Reconciliation Symposium as unfairly one-sided, and Eric DeSobe, after making it clear that he in some way sympathized with me, noted that nothing was being reconciled at the panel on race reconciliation since no one offered any opposing opinions ("Reconciliation requires vigorous debate," January 30). Columnist Christopher Richardson recently commented on how one-sided and unreasonable a later race forum was, noting that Colin Powell was referred to as "a good slave" and that all the panelists shared basically the same sentiments ("Forum called lack of progress to attention," February 13).

At the heart of the problem is the attitude expressed by one student who, when asked why he wasn't attending any of the Symposium events, said something to the effect of "I agree with all the perspectives that are being presented, so I don't think it's necessary for me to go." Such a prejudice in favor of the most popular, most politically correct solution to the world's problems strikes me as anathema to everything for which a university should stand. It seems to me that the university isn't doing its job of getting students to think for themselves, but is rather encouraging them to uncritically recite those ideas which happen to be the trendiest or the most popular, and denounce anyone who dares differ. Sometimes I think that if the prevailing view were that single women over age 30 were all witches needing to be burned at the stake, or that fascism were a more ideal form of government than democracy, then students would unquestioningly agree so long as that's what everyone around them believed.

Ideas always need to be challenged in order for progress to be made, and the *de facto* suppression of the open exchange of ideas on university campuses in the form of political correctness is a problem needing attention, regardless of where one stands on any particular issue.

February 23, 2001

A Balance Must be Struck Between Nature & Man

On Saturday I had the opportunity to listen to Harvard ento-mologist Edward O. Wilson, the founder of sociobiology and one of America's greatest scientists, deliver one of the keynote ad-dresses of the Year of Reconciliation Symposium.

Having previously taken a course on the evolutionary pers-pectives of animal behavior at Emory, I knew that Wilson's pro-motion of the theory that certain animal (and human) behaviors had evolved because of their evolutionary adaptiveness had caused quite a stir among scientific circles. I also took note of the fact that many of the same scientists for whom I suspect the de-fense of leftist ideology outweighs the need for critical rationali-ty, most notably Harvard colleagues Stephen Jay Gould and Ri-chard Lewontin, vehemently attacked the notion of sociobiology when Wilson first published a book on the subject in 1975.

More recently, Wilson has written a book entitled *Consilience*, which discusses the current fragmentation of academia into dis-ciplines that approach similar questions from quite different an-gles, often arriving at mutually contradictory solutions. As an alternative to this approach, Wilson advocates what he terms the "unity of knowledge," in which the social sciences and the natu-ral sciences come together to provide an answer to a given ques-tion that takes all available knowledge into account.

A brief example of such a synthesis would be the theory of gene-culture co-evolution, which holds that *Homo sapiens* have evolved both genetically and culturally, and that the two forms of evolution are linked. Unfortunately, far too many intellec-tuals, public policymakers, and media professionals hold the view that human culture has departed from genes and become a thing unto itself, free from the biological and psychological processes that initiated it. I'm not comfortable with the idea that these very individuals are the ones who draw up public policy, and I share Wilson's dream of an enlightened age in which solu-tions to problems can be envisioned not through the lens of any particular ideology, but rather through a critical examination of the available evidence followed with inductive reasoning.

But the subject of consilience wasn't the topic of Wilson's keynote address Saturday. Rather, he dealt with a topic just as equally deserving of attention: the environment and humanity's responsibility to preserve it. Of all the problems facing mankind, only our answer to this one will have consequences that shape the world hundreds of millennia from now and extend to species beyond our own. It is in solving this problem that we must rise above ideology and approach every potential solution with an open mind and a willingness to change.

The central issue that we must face is: Were it not for humanity, the environment and all the endangered species in it would not be threatened. Yet, were it not for the advances made by humanity, many of us would not enjoy the standard of living frequently taken for granted. Wilson pointed out that Americans consume several times the level of natural resources used by those in developing nations, and mentioned the exponential rate at which the human population is increasing.

Later in his speech, however, he raised the issue of the "slash and burn" destruction of tropical rain forests performed in countries whose citizens require farmland to develop because there is no local economic infrastructure available for them to work as craftsmen or non-agricultural laborers. He then stressed the need for economic assistance to the inhabitants of these nations in order to provide them with alternatives to clearing the tropical rain forests, as well as the need for governments, the private sector, and scientists to work together toward solutions to this environmental problem.

After Wilson's speech, there was a small amount of time allocated for a question-and-answer session. I considered asking him about his thoughts on an apparent problem I saw in providing economic assistance to developing nations, namely the need for living space brought about by the population growth such assistance would encourage. A friend of mine with whom I spoke after the address had thought about asking a similar question of Wilson: If he had to choose between saving human lives and raising the standard of living in developing nations on the one hand or saving the natural environment on the other, which would he choose?

Foreign aid to developing nations and humanitarian support for the poor and malnourished appears to be noble, but if such assistance contains no provisions for controlling population growth in these societies, then not only will more individuals needing assistance continue to be born, but the drain on the natural environment will increase.

If bringing developing nations to First World standards results in a level of raw goods consumption equivalent to the *per capita* level in the United States, then is humanity in fact contributing to its own decline by overtaxing and depleting the natural resources upon which we rely for our existence?

These are tough questions, ones for which ideology often dictates a certain response. Yet true thinkers and scholars must avoid the lure of ideology, consider all angles, and not shy away from critical inquiry while answering these and other questions in the search for a feasible solution to the problems facing the environment.

January 30, 2001

APATHY ELIMINATION: THREE SUGGESTIONS

One frequently hears students complaining about the lack of school spirit at Emory. Student Government Association candidates frequently say that they are going to effectively address this issue but rarely succeed in making any lasting changes. While having too much school spirit could result in a homogeneity that restricts free thought and diversity of opinion, I don't think Emory will be in any danger of being too spirited anytime soon. Likewise, I don't believe that I'm in any danger of being the one to finally bring unity to Emory. So, here are a few ideas for promoting school spirit, do with them what you will:

Drunkenness. Short of adding a football team to give students a common banner under which to unite, the Administration might as well give students a common substance under which to unite. Alcohol has a way of making average music sound awesome, of making average girls seem drop dead gorgeous, and of making the world generally seem like a friendly place. Plan a Reconciliation forum in which University President William M. Chace, former Business School Professor Jeffrey Sonnenfeld, Black Student Alliance President Awenate Cobbina, and myself are all seated together and are only allowed to speak after we've had ten shots of liquor apiece, and you'll see more reconciliation in a matter of minutes than what's occurred all year during this Year of Reconciliation. Of course, excessive alcohol consumption can cause long-term health problems as well as short-term errors in reasoning, judgment, and perception. Nonetheless, its power to make college-aged students come together (no pun intended) should not be ignored or downplayed.

Events that appeal to all. Since Emory lacks a tradition of rallying behind any particular athletic team, I would suggest planning other events that also appeal to everyone. The very few that exist fulfill my first idea quite well (e.g. Dooley's Ball), though ideally alcohol shouldn't be the focus. Some sort of campus-wide fair, open to the surrounding community as well as to students and faculty, would not only generate revenue but would also allow students an opportunity to interact outside the classroom. The events that do occur usually lack a broad appeal. While events that specifically appeal to those of a certain race, ethnicity, religion, sexual orientation, or other group can be valuable in their own right and have their time and place, they do little to build a sense of community. As much as these events may proclaim that "all are invited," "all" rarely come. Indeed some, such as "Comparative Apartheid: South Africa and Israel," may even reduce it (yet should nonetheless be preserved in the interests of academic freedom and free speech).

Mandatory extracurriculars. The only place I've experienced any spirit of the non-liquid variety at this school has been with the Emory swimming and diving team. Ideally, a swim team forms a sort of a fraternity in and of itself, one united not by wealth and alcohol, but rather by hard work and the common pursuit of shared team goals. This year, the men's team motto is "Strength and Honor," taken from the movie *Gladiator*. Those are words that are quickly losing meaning in today's world of smug politicians who lie with a smile and fat international financiers who don't hesitate to betray their country in order to attain personal wealth.

From my own experience, I believe that the number of Emory students who truly understand what it means to work for something greater than themselves over the long term and have experienced and overcome a decent amount of hardship in their lives is rather small, and tends to be highest among foreign students and minorities. Usually, the wealthier a family one comes from, the more a student is provided with everything and the less opportunity he or she has to mature and develop on his or her own. Putting oneself through school, participating in competitive sports, and having to work for long-term goals instead of wallowing in short-term indulgence help turn children into adults, and are things I imagine today's generation of naïve, White college students tend to lack more than in previous generations.

Well, those are three things I believe would help, one on a superficial level, the other two on a progressively deeper and more lasting level. President Chace, I'm ready for those ten shots when you are.

March 9, 2001

IS DIVERSITY REALLY
A STRENGTH?

While I don't doubt that exposure to different cultures, languages, and ways of looking at things can help make one a more refined and broad-minded individual, I question whether ethnic diversity inherently tends to unite individuals, rather than cause division and weakness. I think diversity can contribute positively to a liberal education, providing exposure to differing languages, cultures, religions and ways of viewing the world. Yet, I see no evidence that diversity, in and of itself, strengthens the day-to-day working of a community. Generally speaking, when people who do not share the same language and customs are forced to communicate and interact, friction and misunderstanding result.

The strongest groups of which I've ever been a member have all been fairly homogeneous. Generally speaking, heterogeneity of any type almost always brings with it conflict, dissension, and disagreement. Individuals who lack a shared context find it harder to work together towards common goals. While one can learn much by interacting with those who are different, all other things equal, a homogeneous group will unite more quickly and work together far better than a "diverse" group.

Race relations at Emory would improve if the school had its own culture and set of traditions into which everyone was made to feel a part. A football team would help, as would other traditions. I agree with College sophomore Chris Richardson's recent assessment that the Oxford campus is much more unified because of a sense of shared tradition.

I disagree with Richardson's belief that raising minority enrollment at Emory would help improve race relations. The University could argue that learning to work with people of different races is a skill that young Americans will need in their future lives. All other factors staying the same, raising the level of ethnic diversity, as with increasing any other sort of heterogeneity, weakens the sense of shared tradition and culture students have. This will simply create more opportunities for racial tension.

I am not calling for a reduction in ethnic diversity at this school. I think that exposure to individuals of different backgrounds and cultures is a benefit of the liberal education Emory and other top universities provide. I only wish to state that increasing ethnic diversity will hurt — not help — race relations at Emory.

If there is anything to be learned from conflicts like those in the Middle East or the former Yugoslavia, it's that peaceful coexistence between differing groups may be governmentally or externally imposed for a short while, but such forced imposition merely constitutes a Band-Aid solution. A communist regime held Yugoslavia together by imprisoning those ethnic nationalists who spoke out against it, under provisions similar to the "hate speech" and "intolerance" laws in effect on many American university campuses, as well as imposed on entire populations in Canada and much of Europe. This artificial bliss ended with the fall of communism.

When the Soviet Union fell, it quickly split among ethnic lines. Ethnic groups that wanted but did not immediately gain independence from Russia are now locked in violent conflicts that have lasted for nearly a decade. How many lives would have been saved if Russia had recognized Chechnya's desire to exist autonomously, instead of trying to subdue Chechen freedom fighters?

In the Middle East, the farce referred to as the "Peace Process" has lasted for decades, yet violence remains a part of day-to-day life in that region. Iron-fisted approaches to dealing with radicals on both sides may stop violence for a short while, but I'm convinced the only long-term solution will be a separate Palestinian state so that Palestinians no longer have to deal with Israelis, and Israelis no longer have to deal with Palestinians. Unfortunately, cities like Jerusalem will probably always remain hotbeds of violence unless they are completely controlled and inhabited purely by one side or the other.

America is currently experiencing a demographic shift unprecedented in history, as a result of the loosening of legal immigration standards in the 1960s and massive illegal immigration towards which both the Democrats and the Republicans have turned a blind eye, each party for its own reasons. The possibility of America experiencing the same sort of problems that the former Yugoslavia continues to experience is very real. It is one the Democrats are willing to overlook as long as they can get more votes from new immigrants, and one that Republicans are willing to overlook as long as big business can profit from cheap labor. Unfortunately, not addressing the issue now will result in greater problems down the road.

Will Emory, where most students don't hesitate to pay lip service to the ideals of diversity and multiculturalism, then proceed to self-segregate and hang out in their own ethnic or cultural cliques, serve as a microcosm for the future America?

Name one nation that stayed together and existed in harmony as a multiethnic country for any extended period of time without being compelled to do so by its government, and I might just begin to be convinced that diversity brings people together instead of pushing them apart.

April 24, 2001

"What to Do?"

When I made the decision to stir controversy as a student at Emory, I didn't expect my initial column to be well-received. I expected sharp criticism from faculty, social isolation from peers, and possibly other consequences. However, I didn't write the column merely to stir controversy or to rebel against institutionalized anti-White bigotry (though I do not deny these motives played some role).

Call it youthful naïveté, but I thought my column would do some good in the short-term during the so-called "Year of Reconciliation." I believed (and still believe) that differing opinions are best "reconciled" through reasoned discourse and the free exchange of ideas. I hoped that at least a small number of other students and faculty members at the university would share this opinion. I also hoped that at some point during the year, a moderated "both sides"-type debate would occur on the topic of race differences, at which I could hopefully secure the attendance of like-minded academics.

I learned the hard way that arguing the facts, by itself, rarely changes peoples' minds. I also learned that one's *motive* in pursuing an argument, rather than the actual validity of the argument, plays a large role in whether an argument is convincing.

At parties my column often became a point of conversation. After several beers, many students were willing to admit to me that, yes, race differences were real, and yes, Blacks are generally less intelligent and more prone to crime than Whites, and yes, genes play a significant role in this difference.

But after admitting these things, "What to do?" became the next logical topic of conversation. Here is where the most disagreement occurred. A good number of students stated (or implied) that I acted irresponsibly by failing to explicitly address the "what to do" question after raising the race/IQ/crime issue. They believed that my column only served to inflame racial tension, and that nothing good could come of it.

These students wanted to know what my *motive* was: What

exactly was I hoping to accomplish by starting this controversy? I didn't want to come across as overly fanatical, so I just informed them of my general belief that problems should be openly discussed rather than downplayed and ignored.

Over the past several months, I've received several emails from persons arguing basically the same point; namely, I should not discuss America's problems if I cannot solve them. It seems that the more aware people are of the magnitude of the race problem, the more afraid they are of confronting it. So most remain silent, hoping that somehow we can muddle through with insane policies premised on the falsehood of racial equality — policies that, in the long run, will lead to the dispossession and destruction of the White race as our living spaces are flooded, and our political institutions are taken over, by fast-breeding and hostile non-Whites.

These people are intimidated from discussing the problems of multiracial societies because they can envision no peaceful solution. The advocates of multiracialism claim — through all the channels of the mass media — that talk of racial separatism can lead only to ethnic cleansing and genocide. They are not willing to explore the possibility that different races occupying the same territory can part ways peacefully. And they smuggle in the premise that the ethnic cleansing and genocide of others is too high a price to pay for our own racial survival; i.e., for not becoming victims of ethnic cleansing and genocide ourselves.

I reject the notion that it is irresponsible to discuss racial problems unless one can also come up with a solution. Unfortunately, as with any other major problem, there's no such thing as a quick and easy fix. There's no solution I can suggest that would be easy to accept. But that doesn't mean we can't talk about the problem. In fact, the longer we avoid discussing it, the greater the likelihood of violence. Thus I think the best first step toward solving the race problem is simply for all sides to openly voice their opinions and the reasons they hold them.

Adults generally deal with problems by talking through them in their early stages, rather than keeping their opinions to themselves and then exploding in fury at a later stage, when the problem has grown so large that it can no longer be ignored — and, in some cases, can no longer be solved.

Imagine you are in an intimate relationship that isn't going anywhere, a relationship you know has to end sooner or later, the only question being "when?" Or let's say you have serious problems with your boss at work, problems you know won't go away by themselves.

Do you think it would be a good idea to not share your feelings until you have a concrete plan laid out for what has to be done? Or do you think it would be better to say what's on your mind, and why it is bothering you, as soon as possible?

I think that a better resolution would come about if both parties are able to freely voice what's on their mind as soon as a problem presents itself. This would give them an opportunity to more fully understand one another and hear one another out. Perhaps both parties could come to an understanding and remain friends, or, if they part ways, they can at least do so amicably, with mutual respect, rather than hating one another the rest of their lives.

This principle applies to race relations as well. I think *all* races would be better served by openly voicing mutual grievances. Not speaking up now will only compound the problem in the future, and like most problems, this one won't go away all by itself.

I of course don't think ethnic cleansing and genocide are desirable solutions. But I think the best way to avoid that sort of hatred and bloodshed is to have open discussion about problems. I think virtually any "conflict resolution" councilor would tell two opposing parties the best way to avoid violence is by talking things out.

The truth is, most Whites know something is wrong, no matter how resistant they may be to discussion. In fact, some of those most resistant to discussion are most aware of the problem but are paralyzed by its very magnitude. It is important to keep this in mind, so that we are not too easily discouraged. The first victory is not to sway people to our side, but simply to get them talking.

September 15, 2004

SWIMMING LESSONS

The period from late December until mid-January is a significant time of the year for me. During most of the past ten years, these weeks entailed much more than just celebrating Christmas and the New Year. As a competitive swimmer, they involved hellish three hour swimming workouts under cold, less-than-ideal training conditions. In college, Winter Break ended with the New Year, for on January 2nd the swim team headed down to Boca Raton, Florida, for winter training. During this season of short days and bad weather, it's hard not to think back to my days as a swimmer.

Fortunately, although the workouts were mentally and physically grueling, they were also the climax of the swim season: After winter training the workouts got progressively easier. My teammates and I always felt extremely pleased once we had them under our belt, not only because they were difficult but also because they were necessary for fast performances at the end-of-the-season championship meets. I learned valuable lessons as a swimmer, lessons I find it useful to reflect upon from time to time since they are applicable to just about every endeavor one undertakes in life.

First, individuals differ in natural talent (innate ability) as well as in the amount of effort they are willing to exert to achieve their goals.

A swimmer has little control over his natural aptitude for the sport or for any particular swimming event. Some swimmers are better at shorter distances, others at longer distances. Some are better at freestyle, while others are better at breaststroke. Some are naturally talented and can perform well even with little training, while others might perform poorly even with extensive training and hard work. On the other hand, a swimmer does have control over his level of commitment to the sport. A highly dedicated swimmer plans his life around swim practices, and exerts a lot of effort into each practice. At the other extreme, a slacker only practices when he feels like it, and doesn't push himself when he does.

Swimming is a microcosm for life in this respect. People vary in attractiveness, mental ability, and physical ability. Everyone has a maximum limit in each of these areas, a limit governed by nature. How close one comes to actualizing his potential, however, ultimately depends on how hard he is willing to push himself.

Another important lesson I learned is that while hard work is a prerequisite for success, it doesn't guarantee it.

When a swimmer fails to attain his goals, the first person he must blame is himself. Unless the swimmer went through the season perfectly, attending every practice and pushing himself, there's always room for improvement.

Yet even if there were no room for improvement, one might still fall short of one's self-expectations. That's an unfortunate consequence of living in an unfair, imperfect world. All one can do is react to life's imperfection positively and productively, rather than negatively and destructively.

Such phrases as "Success is a direction, not a location," and "10% of life is what happens, 90% is how you react to it" are all true. You are your own greatest enemy when you give in to defeatist, negative thinking that takes failure as an unalterable judgment on one's worth. This thinking minimizes the chances good things will occur in the future, since it's often followed by a self-fulfilling prophecy like "I'll never do better," "I'm simply no good," or "I can't."

My father once told me that Mussolini ordered the word "impossible" removed from all dictionaries in Italy, since theoretically nothing is impossible. While I have my doubts as to whether this actually occurred, I could see why Mussolini would rhetorically make such a statement.

I don't think I'd go so far as to recommend eliminating the concept of "impossible." It's always best to think objectively and rationally about the choices one must make in life, and sometimes the chance of success is so slim it might as well be considered "impossible." But there's no doubt in my mind that once one has made a decision to pursue a certain goal, one should never think negatively along the path towards achieving it. Irrational optimism is far preferable to irrational pessimism.

When confronted with failure, don't get discouraged, think things will never change, and have this belief turn into a self-fulfilling prophecy. Rather, learn from your mistakes, make the necessary changes, and try again with a positive attitude.

Finally, swimming has taught me the value of persistence and continual effort, rather than sporadic bursts of enthusiasm.

Swimmers who consistently attend five swim practices a week generally have better seasons than those who attend three some weeks, and seven on others. Physically, the body develops better when exercised regularly rather than sporadically. Psychologically, a steady five practices a week causes less stress and anxiety than falling short one week then struggling to catch up the next.

Success in life works in a similar fashion to success in swimming in this regard. A consistent routine pays greater dividends than stop-and-go efforts. This rule holds true for virtually every pursuit one undertakes in life, be it physical, spiritual, or economic. It's a rule particularly relevant to White Nationalists, since we must maximize our chances for success by not yielding to feelings of despair and hopelessness. Our evolutionary background, which required our ancestors to delay gratification and plan ahead for food shortages during winter, gives us an advantage in this regard, an advantage we must exploit.

Swimming not only taught me lessons about how to succeed as an individual. It also taught me about how to be part of a team and strive for the common good. It showed me how being part of a collective can encourage individual pride, initiative, and achievement, and how these can contribute to the collective good.

My fondest memories are of the camaraderie team members shared, especially in the days preceding a meet against a rival school.

Swimmers relied on one another throughout the season, by encouraging each other during workouts and by psyching each other up before and during important swim meets. There were times, during the most difficult training periods of the season, when some swimmers expressed negative attitudes. But these were also the times when the most dedicated and disciplined members of the team were able to shine. These tough periods allowed leaders to emerge who encouraged and set an example for younger or less disciplined team members.

Both positive and negative thinking are contagious, and the most charismatic and enthusiastic swimmers on the team worked along with the coaches to ensure negative attitudes didn't prevail. During Winter Training, for instance, there were plenty of things one *could* complain about: having to wake up at 5:30 am, having to train outdoors on cold and rainy days, having to endure hard, long distance sets, etc. But since team members didn't have outside obligations to worry about (Winter Training occurs between semesters), no one could say that anyone had it "harder" than anyone else. Add to this the fact that guys who complained would have to do so in the presence of girls who *weren't* complaining, and one can see why negative attitudes were quickly squelched.

Ultimately, the swimmers of both sexes who consistently worked hard and didn't lament about how difficult things were, earned the respect of their peers. Others then tried to emulate this behavior. The team grew more united as leaders emerged, and unspoken competitions began to see who was more dedicated.

Explicit rivalry amongst team members was encouraged. During challenging sets, swimmers in adjacent lanes would often race against one another. Typically the guys openly challenged and playfully taunted one another. The girls, on the other hand, usually encouraged each other in a less aggressive fashion, although on longer distance sets, where significant overlap in ability between the sexes existed, a girl might taunt a guy she thought she could beat.

Needless to say, this sort of one-upmanship ensured swimmers gave their full effort during sets. It also prepared swimmers for real competition against opposing teams. Finally, it brought the team closer together, because this intra-team competition helped each individual to perform his or her best later on, when it really mattered. The team was a collection of self-motivated individuals united under a common cause (namely, beating all the other teams at the end of the season), and by competing amongst ourselves we ensured the team as a whole would be the strongest it possibly could be at the end of the season.

Probably the biggest example of intra-team rivalry was competition for relay spots. Relays consisted of four swimmers, whom the coaches decided would perform best based upon previous times as well as performance in practice. Needless to say, swimmers who weren't chosen felt disappointed in some sense, but understood the reasoning behind the decision and so knew what they had to do if they wanted to represent the team in the future. They wanted the team to perform at its best, even if that meant acknowledging individual deficiencies.

Before big meets, the men's and women's teams would usually meet separately in their respective locker rooms, and we would wait for the coaches to come by and announce the relay teams. Then either the coach or one of the more senior swimmers would offer a few motivational things to say. The team would then do a cheer (one of several during the course of the meet), come out to the pool, and warm-up. Team members fed off of each other's enthusiasm, and strong performances by individual swimmers during the meet helped inspire others to also perform well.

To me, the swim team represents the ideal interplay between individualism and collectivism. Competition between individuals on the team helped both the individual swimmer as well as the team as a whole. The interest of the group was more important than the interest of the individual, but this ordering helped ensure both the individual and the group were the best they could possibly be. Any individual swimmer had his or her strengths and his or her weaknesses, and even the most dedicated swimmers needed others to inspire them occasionally. But acting together, individuals could accomplish and become far more than they ever could on their own.

It would be naïve to think that a totally heterogeneous collection of people can become a community simply by adopting common goals. Common goals cannot be adopted by those who do not already share something in common. Common goals presuppose a common heritage. Not just a common cultural heritage, but also a common genetic heritage. The teams I was a part of were overwhelmingly White. Swimming is still an overwhelmingly White sport in the US. The character of the teams and of the sport as a whole would inevitably have changed with the presence of a large number of non-Whites, just as large numbers of non-Whites have transformed the character and team unity of such sports as football, baseball, and basketball.

But given a common heritage, ideally a nation should be like a swim team, its citizens just as united under a common vision of the future, competing with one another to ensure the nation is the best it can be in its competitions with the rest of the world.

These international rivalries need not be violent and destructive either. There are also peaceful rivalries that contribute to the continued perfection of culture and evolution of life. I am thinking not of the arms race, but the space race. Not of war games, but Olympic games. The competition between patrons of art, not of war.

January 31 & February 13, 2004

ELUSIVE AMERICAN
VIRTUES & THE OLYMPICS

Ahh, the Olympics. It's a shame they can't take place in Atlanta more often.

During these few fleeting moments that come around only once every four years, athletes who have worked their way to the top of their sports enjoy the international spotlight, and a select few experience what it's like to stand at the very top.

Millions of people deify their country's Olympic champions, if only for a short period of time. Why do we do this?

The qualities that contribute to the making of an Olympian are the same qualities Americans (especially young people) too often lack. Society glorifies instant gratification, but doesn't do enough to stress the values that really determine success or failure in life. Although sex, drugs, booze, rock 'n' roll, and easy money aren't necessarily bad, too often these things fall into the hands of people who don't understand the meaning of words like "responsibility," "delayed gratification," and "commitment." This holds particularly true on college campuses.

Don't misunderstand me. I like to drink just as much as the next guy, and I certainly wouldn't mind winning a million dollars on TV. Each of the things I listed above brings (or would bring) me great pleasure, while it lasted. And that's exactly the point I want to make: The euphoria obtained from each and every one of the things listed above is fleeting at best.

Only feats achieved despite adversity, against all odds, and at great hardship to the doer can bring joy and a sense of accomplishment decades after being performed. While these feats vary in magnitude and extend well beyond the realm of sports, it is in sporting events (particularly amateur ones) that we can most readily observe the qualities that lead to success in all areas of life.

As a case in point, although this school is greatly lacking in spirit, I can say from experience that there is a lot of spirit on our swim team, and I'm guessing there's no shortage of it among the other sports teams as well. Why? Because anyone who has stuck with a sport like swimming or cross country or rowing or any other sport that requires daily training to prepare for only a handful of big performances during the season, knows that to achieve shared end-of-season goals, everyone must delay gratification and work together. To quote the late Vince Lombardi, "Once you agree upon the price you and your team must pay for success, it enables you to ignore the minor hurts, the opponent's pressure, and the temporary failures." The result is team bonding and a sense of direction and purpose, which in turn leads to high spirits.

Although the swim team get the spotlight during the University Athletic Association meet and at Division III nationals, the time to really see us at our best, the time when our character really shines through, is during the hard sets we swim throughout the season. At a typical Saturday morning long course practice during the heart of the season, the looks on peoples' faces as our coach reads the main set speak volumes. Except for the one or two people who still exhibit the effects of some lingering intoxication from the night before, everyone has pretty much the same fixed stare, and so I know everyone's probably thinking just what I'm thinking: "Why the hell am I here when I could be sleeping in?"

Yet, deep down, everyone who's on the team can answer that question. We're there because we all have goals we'd like to reach and are thus willing to sacrifice the easy choice for the harder one.

And it's because of this deep-down knowledge that an onlooker will observe more than just swimmers going up and down the pool lap after lap. He or she will also hear us challenging one another (in no uncertain terms) to swim faster as we race against one another towards the end of a tough set. After the set is done we feel a shared sense of accomplishment, and we're ready to start our Saturdays knowing we've come one step closer to achieving our goals. This jump-start on the day rolls over into other tasks we have to complete, and helps us feel less guilty about engaging in certain "instantaneously gratifying" behaviors Saturday night.

I'm not encouraging everyone to take up swimming, but I am encouraging self-discipline, commitment, and dedication. The Olympics epitomize the great triumphs these values can bring about. Perhaps only a select few have the innate potential to achieve victory in the Olympics, but we can all set goals and dare to strive for them. After all, in the end, what you get by achieving your goals is not half as important as the person you become in the process.

September 22, 2000

THE CHRIST-KILLERS TODAY

I am not a Christian, but justice requires me to protest the campaign against Mel Gibson's *The Passion of the Christ*, a campaign largely orchestrated and executed by Jews, along with some servile Gentile lackeys.

The Passion is not a Hollywood movie, "Hollywood" being the Jew-dominated American film industry that was uninterested in making or financing or distributing the film, even though it was a surefire hit. Instead, *The Passion* was made in Italy and bankrolled by Mel Gibson personally to the tune of $30 million. If Jews had as much control over the global film industry as they do the American, and if Mel Gibson were a penniless artist, *The Passion* never would have been made. Now that he has made it, Hollywood's Jewish moguls are sending Gibson a message: "I won't hire him. I won't support anything he's part of."[1]

When *The Passion* could not be stopped, Jews around the world organized a campaign of threats and intimidation, hoping to bully Gibson into allowing them to shape the movie. Their main spokesman is Abraham Foxman of the Anti-Defamation League of B'nai B'rith (which means "Brotherhood of the Circumcised"). True to its long history of criminality and deceit, the ADL's allies and operatives stole a copy of the script, sneaked into advance screenings by pretending to be Christian clergymen, and violated signed agreements not to disclose what they saw prior to the film's release. Then, true to its long history of defamation, the ADL proceeded to smear Mel Gibson and attack his movie. The ADL's website has also targeted impressionable teens with special anti-*Passion* propaganda. Foxman has even gone so far as to demand that the Pope denounce *The Passion* for being scripturally inaccurate and theologically unorthodox. But somehow I doubt he is sincere in his defense of Christian orthodoxy.

Since *The Passion* was released in the United States on Ash

---

[1] Quoted in Sharon Waxman, "New Film May Harm Gibson's Career," *New York Times*, February 26, 2004,
http://www.nytimes.com/2004/02/26/movies/26GIBS.html

Wednesday, Jews and their tools have done everything they can to keep audiences away.

Ugly demonstrations have been staged.

"Hate Crimes" investigators have been called, and a petition has been started imploring John Ashcroft to take action against the film's creators "for violation of state and federal hate crime statutes in the purposeful encouragement of anti-Semitic violence." (Since no actual crimes have been committed, we see quite clearly that the real purpose of "Hate Crimes" laws is to create a category of Thought Crimes, and apparently Christianity will be one of them.)

Jews in England, France, and Israel — and probably in other countries where it is illegal to criticize Jews but not Christians — are working to ban *The Passion*. To strike fear into the hearts of the superstitious, to whom this movie will have the greatest appeal, the death of an elderly woman watching *The Passion* was turned into national news. Never mind that such a death was probably a statistical inevitability given the vast numbers of people who have seen the film. Somehow, I do not think it will be national news when someone dies watching the next Spielberg or Bruckheimer flick.

The negative reviews all sound like they are from the same script, probably because they are. *The Passion* is condemned as too violent and bloody, as if that mattered to critics before. It is condemned as historically inaccurate, as if that mattered to critics. It is condemned for being scripturally inaccurate and theologically unorthodox, as if that mattered to critics. It is condemned for being boring, and in foreign languages with subtitles, as if that mattered to the people who pimped for every pretentious French "art" flick in history.

The Passion has also been smeared as "pornographic," which means a lot from the type that hailed movies like *The Last Temptation of Christ* and *Dogma* and defended Andres Serrano's "Piss Christ" (a plastic crucifix immersed in urine and cow's blood) and Chris Ofili's elephant dung-encrusted Madonna as works of art and worthy recipients of tax dollars.

The Passion has even been called a "snuff film." Well, I'm sure the critics are betters judges of this than I. But if a "snuff film" is simply any movie in which a murder is presented, then practically every Hollywood film is a snuff film. And if a "snuff film" is one in which a real or pretended murder is found to be sexually arousing, then the accusation says more about the accusers than about *The Passion*. So too the claim that the film is "sadomasochistic."

Of course I look forward to seeing these critics apply their new-found scruples to the trash produced by Hollywood. But I won't hold my breath.

The main objection to *The Passion* is that it portrays "the Jews" as responsible for the death of Jesus, and by "responsible" the critics mean *collectively* responsible. But this accusation is ambiguous. Does it refer to *all Jews*, or just all Jews *then*, or all Jews *since then*?

The Passion does not portray *all* Jews as responsible for the death of Jesus, for it does not portray *all Jews then* as responsible. Indeed, Jesus, his mother, and his followers were all Jews. Simon of Cyrene, who helped Jesus carry the cross, was a Jew, but he was not responsible because he was not a willing participant. Jerusalem, not to mention the whole Mediterranean world, was filled with Jews who took no part in the torture and execution of Jesus. Indeed, most Jews were completely unaware that it was happening. No, the only Jews who are shown to be responsible for the death of Jesus are Caiaphas, the High Priest, and some — but certainly not all — of his colleagues.

But some Jews *were* responsible for the death of Jesus. To the extent that we know anything historical about the death of Jesus, we know that. That is what the New Testament says. That is what Flavius Josephus says. That is what the Talmud says. There is no way that Mel Gibson could have made the movie without showing who was responsible for the death of Jesus, which is why Foxman and company preferred it not be made at all.

Does *The Passion* support the view that *all Jews since then* are responsible for the death of Jesus? Yes and no. The crux of the issue is Matthew 27:25: "And all the people answered, 'His blood be on us and on our children!'" Gibson's Jewish critics demanded that he remove this line from *The Passion*. But the line is in the movie only because it is in the Bible, so the demand that it be removed from the movie is tantamount to the demand that it be removed from the Bible. And since Christians believe that the Bible is the Word of God, censoring the Bible is censoring God.

Jews do not have the power to censor God. Not yet, anyway. But they did, apparently, have the power to censor *The Passion*. Gibson originally included "His blood be on us and on our children," but since it would have been odd for a whole crowd to chant it, he gave the line to Caiaphas.

"For fear of the Jews," however, Gibson removed the subtitle. So unless one knows Aramaic and knows where the line belongs, it is as good as gone. "'I wanted it in,' [Gibson] said. 'My brother said I was wimping out if I didn't include it. But, man, if I included that in there, they'd be coming after me at my house. They'd come to kill me.'"[2]

As Alex Linder puts it so memorably, Jesus is the only Jew Christians are not afraid of offending. Let's hope that Mel Gibson has a change of heart and decides to put what he supposedly believes to be God's words back into *The Passion* when it is released on DVD.

Gibson, however, is not the only Christian who is willing to tamper with God's words. After more than half a century of post-Holocaust Jewish propaganda and lobbying, most Christian theologians claim that the real meaning of "His blood be on us and on our children" is that we are *all* guilty of Christ's crucifixion: Pilate, the Jews, you, and me. But this patent misreading ignores the line's context:

Pilate said to them, "Then what shall I do with Jesus who is called Christ?" They all said, "Let him be crucified." And he said, "Why, what evil has he done?" But they shouted all the more, "Let him be crucified." So when Pilate saw that he was gaining nothing, but rather that a riot was beginning, he took water and washed his hands before the crowd, saying, "I am innocent of this man's blood; see to it yourselves." And all the people answered, "His blood be on us and on our children!" (Matthew 27:22-25).

---

[2] http://en.wikipedia.org/wiki/The_Passion_of_the_Christ

It is only after Pilate says that he is not going to kill Jesus that the Jews say that they will take responsibility, and not just for themselves, but for their children as well. The sense is clearly disjunctive: *either* Pilate *or* the Jews can take responsibility, and the Jews take it. The sense is not conjunctive, not: *both* Pilate *and* the Jews take responsibility.

One could argue that Pilate really does bear some responsibility for the murder of Jesus, for he could have prevented it. But the scriptures also make it clear that he deemed it better to sacrifice Jesus to the mob rather than to risk many more deaths in another Jewish rebellion. So even if Pilate could have prevented the murder of Jesus, one could argue that he was not *obligated* to do so; therefore, he was not negligent in handing Jesus over.

But even if Pilate bears some responsibility, that does not implicate the rest of the human race. I, for one, am not responsible for the murder of Jesus. I did not howl for his blood with the mob. I did not scourge him. I did not crown him with thorns. I did not nail him to the cross. I wasn't even born then.

The "we're all guilty" misreading seems plausible to Christians because they believe that Christ died to save us all. (One has to question the sincerity of Jews who tout this misinterpretation, however, for it only makes sense if Jesus really was the Messiah.) But even if Jesus died to save us all, that does not mean that all of us murdered him. Something done *for me* is not necessarily done *by me*.

But what about the claim that not only the Jews who were present, but also their children, are responsible for the murder of Jesus?

First, it does not imply that *all* Jews since then are responsible, only the children of the mob that urged Jesus be crucified. But since there is no way of determining which Jews are descended from that mob and which are not, it makes all Jews since then at least suspects in the murder of Jesus.

Second, the children of the mob are guilty only on the assumption that guilt is hereditary and collective. Now, from my own secular and scientific perspective, the notion of collective and hereditary guilt is pure nonsense. But from a Christian point of view, it is quite plausible. For what is "Original Sin" if not a collective and hereditary guilt for the transgressions of Adam and Eve? So even though I do not believe that Jews are collectively and hereditarily guilty for the murder of Jesus, *perhaps Christians should*. At least there is ample material both in the Bible and in the Christian tradition for constructing such a doctrine.

Two things give plausibility to such a fable. First is the uncanny collective-mindedness of Jews. It is hard to treat them like individuals because they seldom think or act like them. Second is the long history of Jewish hatred of Christianity, which over the centuries has given rise to terrible persecutions whenever Jews have gained political power. The Acts of the Apostles record the persecution of Jesus's earliest followers. Saul, called Paul, was on his way to Damascus to persecute its Christians when he had his famous vision of Jesus. The *Acta Sanctorum* also records a number of instances in which Jews instigated Roman persecutions of Christians.

Israel Shamir, in recent article entitled "Freak Factory," mentions other persecutions.[3] In 135 AD, followers of the Jewish rebel Simon Bar Kokhba massacred Christians in Palestine. In 519 AD, Yusuf Zu Nawas, the Jewish ruler of Himyar in present-day Yemen, massacred Christians and destroyed churches. In 529 AD, the Jews of Palestine took advantage of the Samaritan uprising to massacre Christians and destroy churches. They did the same in 614 AD, during the invasion of the Persian Emperor Chosroes II.

But the greatest Jewish persecution of Christians took place less than a century ago after the Bolsheviks seized control of the Russian Empire. Virtually all the Bolshevik leaders were Jews (like Trotsky), part-Jews (like Lenin), or married to Jews (like Stalin). The Bolsheviks quickly made anti-Semitism a crime and anti-Christianity state policy. Churches were closed, looted, destroyed; thousands of priests and monks were imprisoned, tortured, murdered. And, in the decades of ever-mounting terror that followed, millions, then tens of millions, of Christians perished at the hands and on the orders of largely Jewish killers.

---

[3] http://www.israelshamir.net/English/Freak_Factory.htm

I wish Christians would keep these crimes in mind the next time a Jew begins a dolorous litany of Christian persecutions of his people. I grant that Jews and Christians trading atrocity stories and demanding apologies from one another for the crimes of their co-religionists would be a preposterous spectacle. But it is far better than the spectacle of Christians always turning the other cheek to Jews, with their aggressive claims of victimhood and absurd pretenses of blamelessness.

Jewish hatred of Christianity is not just a matter of isolated outbursts of persecution. Indeed, these outbursts are merely symptoms of a deep and abiding hatred codified in Jewish religious writings and practices. Israel Shahak gives an interesting overview of these writings and practices in his book *Jewish History, Jewish Religion: The Weight of Three Thousand Years.*[4]

The Talmud, for instance, claims that Jesus' legal father was cuckolded not by the Holy Spirit but by his best man, that Jesus was conceived while his mother was menstruating and thus "impure," that he was a sexual pervert, a black magician, an idolater, and is being punished in hell in a vat of boiling excrement. The Talmud also claims that Jesus was tried by a religious court for idolatry, inciting other Jews to idolatry, and defying religious authority, that he was condemned to death by stoning, and that he was eventually hanged (perhaps on a cross). (Maybe Mel Gibson should have quoted the Talmud instead of Matthew 27:25.)

Similar claims are found in the Toledot Yeshu, which according to Shamir was after the Bible the most widely circulated Jewish book in the Middle Ages. There Jesus is said to be the illegitimate child of Mary, the wife of a perfumer, and a Roman soldier named Pandera; he went to Egypt where he learned black magic; he returned to Israel to lead the Jews into idolatry; he was arrested and tried by the Sanhedrin, condemned to death, pilloried for forty days, then stoned and hanged (again, this may mean hanged on a cross).

Hatred of Christianity is also expressed in Jewish prayers.

---

[4] Israel Shahak, *Jewish History, Jewish Religion: The Weight of Three Thousand Years* (London: Pluto Press, 1994). Available online at http://radioislam.org/historia/shahak/english.htm

According to Shahak, "In the most important section of the weekday prayer — the 'eighteen blessings' — there is a special curse, originally directed against Christians, Jewish converts to Christianity and other Jewish heretics: 'And may the apostates have no hope and all the Christians perish instantly'" (p. 92). A Jew when seeing a large number of Jews is instructed to praise God, but when he sees a large number of Christians he is supposed to utter a curse. The same applies to buildings: According to the Talmud, when a Jew sees a Christian building, he must ask God to destroy it. When he sees a Christian building in ruins, he is to thank God for destroying it. Later, according to Shahak, this practice came to be applied specifically to churches and crucifixes and was embellished by spitting three times (p. 93). A curse directed specifically at Jesus asks that his name be blotted out altogether. The Talmud also enjoins Jews to burn any copies of the New Testament that come into their hands, and according to Shahak, hundreds of copies of the New Testament were publicly burned in Jerusalem on March 23, 1980 by a state-subsidized Jewish religious organization (p. 21).

Most Jews, of course, do not believe in their God or observe his more absurd and evil commandments. That is to their credit. Some Jews are actually "for" Jesus. Others are indifferent. A few are even willing to examine hateful Jewish attitudes and actions toward Christians self-critically.

But still: It is hard not to see the ugly campaign against Mel Gibson and *The Passion* as merely the latest incident in a long, dark tradition of Jewish anti-Christian bigotry, a bigotry that continues to flourish despite the withering of its religious roots. If Jews today wish to shake the absurd accusation that they are congenital Christ-killers, they should not behave like they are willing to crucify him all over again.

Will *The Passion* increase anti-Semitism? Probably not. Will the Jewish campaign against *The Passion* increase anti-Semitism? Probably so, although the ADL can be trusted to lay all the blame on Mel Gibson and none on itself. After all, the main cause of anti-Semitism is Jewish behavior. Specifically, the behavior that ensues when you stand between a Jew and something he wants, or wants to destroy. Just try it. Rachel Corrie did. The personal attacks, dishonesty, and assaults on one's intellectual liberty quickly become hateful.

But Jewish groups like the ADL have a vested interest in whipping up both anti-Semitism and anti-Christian bigotry. It reinforces Jewish group identity and creates barriers to assimilation.

Furthermore, Jewish groups have been alarmed at the growth of anti-Jewish attitudes and incidents in recent years. In Europe, these are due in large part to increased awareness of Jewish evildoing in Palestine. In the United States, they arise largely from 9/11 and the ensuring wars in Afghanistan and Iraq, which awoke many Americans to the folly of allowing Jews to control our foreign policy and corrupt our political leadership.

The campaign against *The Passion*, however, establishes Mel Gibson as a handy scapegoat for future anti-Jewish sentiments and actions, which will only increase as more people become aware of the evil that Jews do.

March 12, 2004

FANTASIZING FASCISM

Sylvia Plath once wrote that "Every woman adores a Fascist." I wish this were true. It is true, however, that a lot of women fantasize about fascists. These fantasies need not be sexual either.

A case in point is Alice Kaplan, a professor of French whose book *French Lessons* was published by the University of Chicago Press in 1993. Kaplan recalls childhood experiences that had a profound effect on her view of the world. She also describes a number of fantasies she had throughout her life. Although she herself makes no link between her fantasies and her childhood experiences, close examination shows that her experiences shaped her fantasies, and her fantasies influenced her behavior in later life.

Nowhere is this clearer than in her fascination with two French fascist writers, Louis-Ferdinand Céline and Maurice Bardèche. Ultimately Kaplan's interest stems from childhood experiences connected with her father, a lawyer in the Nuremberg tribunals, and the fantasies that arose from these experiences. (Although *French Lessons* is ostensibly about one woman's romance with the French language, the cover is a picture from the Nuremberg tribunals.)

Kaplan's first fantasy (relevant to her later interest in fascism) occurred as she grew up in a Republican, gentile neighborhood. The previous owners of the house are said to have left a detective's report lying on the dining room radiator, apparently to remind the Kaplan family that their neighbors didn't want any more Jews in the neighborhood. This, Kaplan claims, is her first exposure to anti-Semitism, and it made a profound impression on her: "This episode sat in the back of my mind as I grew up. I watched us. We were on trial, being upright for the neighborhood."

This all seems implausible. What, exactly, were the detectives hired to investigate? Did the *goyim* need a detective to determine that a family named Kaplan was Jewish? This is a child's vague understanding of detective work, which is why I label the episode a fantasy.

Later, while searching through her father's drawers, Kaplan

discovered photographs of concentration camp victims. Her first view of dead bodies made a lasting impression. "They didn't look human," she says. She fantasized about shocking her classmates with the photos, even the most gruesome, because, says Kaplan, "I missed my father. I was trying to do what he would do, be like him." (Kaplan will be delighted to know that small children all over the world are now forced to view such gruesome photos in mandatory Holocaust education programs.)

The death of Kaplan's father played an important role in her identity formation. She recalls going fishing with him just before he died, and her brother having told her: "Daddy knows the places in the lake where the fishes like to go." Kaplan mentions her brother's remark because it serves as a metaphor for her father's involvement in Nuremberg: he went to Germany to catch the Nazis responsible for the crimes depicted in the photographs.

When Kaplan asks her mother what happens to people after they die, her mother responded, "Jews do not believe in an afterlife. We believe people live on through their achievements." This sets off a number of fantasies about "living on" and being reunited with her father. This spurred her to complete 60 book reports for her third grade class that year. Her lifelong interest in French language and culture, and her attempts to understand French fascists and literary geniuses (in Céline's case they were one and the same), also seem shaped by fantasies of "living on" through her achievements.

Another noteworthy fantasy in Kaplan's childhood occurs after her father chases down and kills a bat in the family's summer home. Her father "saves" her from the bat, ultimately by squashing it against a wall. After the bat was dead, Kaplan told her mother she wanted to see it. Her mother replied: "Now why in the world would you even want to see such a thing? Bats carry horrible diseases." Recollecting the split second when she saw the bat, Kaplan tells us "it had a human face."

Of course Kaplan didn't really see a human face on the bat. This is just a fantasy. But this fantasy influences her later studies of the French literary fascists Céline and Bardèche. Although her peers told her that Céline, like the bat, carried the "horrible disease" of anti-Semitism and thus should not be studied (unlike the corpses of the presumed-to-be-Jewish concentration camp victims), Kaplan wanted to see Céline's human face. She was convinced he had a human face because, of course, the bat had a human face. (There are many reasons to study Céline, who is one of the great writers of the twentieth century and one of the many great minds attracted to fascism, but this is surely the strangest on record.)

Yet for all his genius, Céline still had evil, bat-like qualities. Kaplan tells of Milton Hindus, a fellow Jew and a professor of literature, who was also fascinated with Céline. In the last letter Hindus received from Céline, he joked about having sex with Jewish girls at Brandeis: "They'd be in the clouds, those Brandeis girls, getting screwed by a Nazi, even an old one . . . just like in Buchenwald."

Personally, I would like to see this letter before believing it. Was it real, or just a fantasy? I don't doubt that Céline could write such things. His anti-Semitic books of the 1930s and 1940s were so extreme that even the Nazis banned them. But I would like to see the context. I very much doubt that Nazis screwed Jews in the concentration camps. The whole point of Nazism was to prevent the mingling of Aryan and non-Aryan genes. There were strict rules against sex with Jews, and harsh punishments for transgressors. But I don't doubt that Jews fantasized about being screwed by Nazis—and not just for purposes of anti-Nazi propaganda—and I wonder if Céline was referring to those fantasies. Seeing the quote in context could clear that up.

Kaplan—as a Jew, as the daughter of a Nuremberg lawyer, and as the discoverer of shocking photographs in her daddy's drawer—was predictably revolted by Céline's alleged statements. She was torn, because Céline is the kind of man her father sent to the gallows in Nuremberg, yet she also admired his literary genius. Interestingly, Kaplan's response to this conflict was to shoot the messenger. She got angry at Hindus, whom she believed provoked Céline to anger. In her eyes, it was Hindus, not Céline, who was responsible for the letter that destroyed her fantasy image of Céline's perfection as a writer. (Hindus may well have been responsible, which is why I would love to see the letter.)

In the early 1980s, Kaplan interviewed Maurice Bardèche. She was surprised at Bardèche's cordiality and kindness, and even laughed with him a few times. In her mind, however, she imagined how her father would advise her to treat Bardèche. She tried to interview him the way her father interviewed Nazis at Nuremberg. (She does not mention the use of torture.) Still, she did not discuss her Jewish identity in order not to destroy her fantasy of Bardèche as Hindus destroyed her fantasy of Céline. Likewise, Bardèche did not bring the topic up out of politeness. By the end of the interview, "Bardèche had ceased to be the person whose most deeply felt ideas horrified me."

Unfortunately, this fantasy too was shattered by a letter where Bardèche frankly discussed his anti-Semitic views. Bardèche tried the soften the blow, telling her "I am afraid that [my letter] might cause you pain . . . I have much sympathy and confidence in you . . . you must try to understand." Perhaps Bardèche was simply an old man who wanted an honest biography written about himself and his ideas, and who hoped that Kaplan could see past their ideological differences.

If so, he was mistaken. Kaplan's reaction was a flashback to the concentration camp photos she saw as a child, a memory "so powerful in my imagination that I often think it the basis of my entire sense of history." Again, she recalls the image of her father killing "bats." Deeply offended and hurt by Bardèche's frank anti-Semitism, Kaplan retaliated by portraying him as "evil and monstrous" in her book on fascism. Later she fantasized about going back to Bardèche's home and telling him off.

It is hard to fathom why the University of Chicago Press deemed Alice Kaplan's memoir worthy of publication. She is an educated woman, but no intellectual giant or innovator, just a professor of French. Kaplan's lack of intellectual rigor and objectivity is remarkable. So too is the brazenness with which she flaunts them. She seems to lack a scholar's conscience altogether. One can only conclude that her other writings are worthless. But if Kaplan is a typical case, then *French Lessons* is at least valuable for documenting the extreme subjectivism and penchant for fantasies—some of them quite colorful, but most of them just banal or sick—that vitiate Jewish discussions of fascism.

February 6, 2004

WAGNER:
DESECRATED BUT NOT DEFEATED

Recently I went to the San Francisco Opera's new production of Richard Wagner's *The Flying Dutchman* (*Der Fliegende Holländer*), and I thought it was worth sharing my reactions, since they relate to larger issues.

It was the first time I had seen *The Flying Dutchman* performed. I had heard Wagner's dark and surging overture, but I had only a general idea of the themes of the story. I decided not to read the synopsis in the program, because I did not want to spoil the unfolding of the story by peeking at the end.

Unfortunately, the story was spoiled for me by stage director Nikolaus Lehnhoff in collaboration with set designer Raimund Bauer, costume designer Andrea Schmidt-Futterer, and choreographer Denni Sayers. Their production was a travesty and a desecration of Wagner, by turns distracting, ridiculous, and downright unintelligible.

Wagner's opera is set along the coast of Norway in the eighteenth or nineteenth century. Lehnhoff's production seems to be set in some sort of vast industrial cargo hold populated by post-apocalyptic mutants, a setting that renders Wagner's talk of sailing ships and spinning wheels jarringly anachronistic.

I am told that in traditional productions, the settings are the deck of a sailing ship, the hall in the house of Daland, the ship's Captain, and a village wharf. In Lehnhoff's production, there is only a vast box, with riveted steel walls, dressed in only slightly different ways for different scenes, with a translucent scrim always hanging between the stage and the audience. This scrim is emblematic of the whole production: Instead of realizing Wagner's genius on stage, it gets between the audience and the artwork, distracting our attention and muddling our understanding.

I imagine that in traditional productions the sailors are dressed like sailors of the time. Since the music for their choruses is filled with humor and high spirits, I imagine that the choreographers instructed them to swagger a bit and swing from the riggings like the nimble young men they are supposed to be. In Lehnhoff's production, they are dressed in bulky silver-colored suits that made them look like fire hydrants clad in Samurai armor, costumes that reduced their movements to ungainly waddling and stiff, mechanical gestures that clashed with the spirit and feel of the music.

I imagine that in traditional productions, the Norwegian maidens in Captain Daland's hall are all thin, pretty young women—I know that is a lot to ask for in the opera world—with fair complexions and rosy cheeks. Their long blonde hair is probably braided, and they are probably wearing long peasant dresses. They sit at spinning wheels spinning wool and singing about their boyfriends. Wagner's sunny music calls to mind graceful feminine forms and gestures and flowing hair and dresses. In Lehnhoff's production, however, the maidens look from the waist up like mutant Geishas and from the waist down like the Daleks from *Doctor Who* Instead of spinning wool, some of them just spin like tops, while the others move their arms in jerky, robotic gestures. Again, the whole scene clashes with the setting and the spirit of the music.

At least Captain Daland and Mary, the nurse of Daland's daughter, Senta, both look human. But they look decidedly un-Norwegian, with masses of brown, frizzy, Negroid hair.

But oddly enough, Senta, who is the heroine of the tale, wears what looks like a costume from a traditional production. And not only does she look human—not to mention thin and beautiful—she is decidedly Nordic, the role being sung by Swedish soprano Nina Stemme. The Dutchman too wears what appears to be a period costume, and his role was sung by Finnish bass baritone Juha Uusitalo.

I suppose I should be grateful for these lapses into good taste, but they so jarringly clashed with the rest of the production's perverse and irritating style that they just made me resent it all the more. Like a well-characterized villain, bad art can almost be redeemed if it at least has integrity, a unity of vision and style. Lehnhoff's production lacks even that.

Lehnhoff's aesthetic crimes go far beyond laughable and distracting costumes and sets. His staging actually makes significant parts of the story unintelligible.

In a traditional staging, I imagine that the Dutchman makes his entrance after his ship pulls up alongside Captain Daland's ship in the dead of night. In Lehnhoff's production, the Dutchman simply walks through a door—along with a puff of smoke and a blaze of light and a mysterious rotating propeller effect—and steps onto the deck of Daland's ship. For all I knew, the Dutchman was already on Daland's ship and was part of his crew. Only later did I realize that he had come from another ship. The entrance was certainly dramatic, but needlessly confusing. (The drama was heightened by the mirror-like polish of the stage, but when the characters were duplicated by their reflections, they looked like a deck of singing playing cards.)

The Dutchman then launched into his riveting aria "Die Frist ist um" ("The Time is Up"), where he describes his tormented life condemned to wander the oceans, longing for death, seeking death, but condemned to live on in solitude until Judgment Day, when the dead will arise and he will finally attain the annihilation for which he longs. (This is a clear inversion of the Christian scheme and shows an almost Buddhist outlook.)

Later we learn that the Dutchman's only chance for redemption before Judgment Day is if he can find a woman who will love him until death. Every seven years, he is allowed to come ashore to search for salvation (= annihilation) through love, and the time has come for another attempt, although the Dutchman's search for love has failed so many times that he is not optimistic.

Juha Uusitalo's voice was magnificent, his German understandable, and his performance deeply moving. For a while, I forgot all about Lehnhoff's perverse production and was swept up in the beauty of the music and the drama of the story. I could not help but identify with the Dutchman's loneliness and his longing for salvation through love, not to mention his constant disappointment.

Another serious lapse in the production comes in Act II, which is set in the Captain Daland's hall. In this act, we are introduced to the heroine, Senta, who is Daland's daughter. We learn that Senta has been infatuated by a fairy tale since childhood. A portrait of the story's hero hangs on the wall. Senta tells his story in another celebrated aria, "Johohoe, Traft ihr das Schiff" ("Johohoe, Have You Seen the Ship"). I found the story puzzling until about half way through the aria (which is quite long), when it dawned on me that she was telling other aspects of the story of the Dutchman.

In a sensible production, I would have known that immediately, because there would have been a portrait of the Dutchman hanging on the wall, a portrait that the audience could clearly identify as the Dutchman. In Lehnhoff's production, the picture is referred to but not shown. This was a needless cause of confusion.

The closest thing to the picture in Lehnhoff's production is a huge shadow of the Dutchman projected on the scrim, which was a nice dramatic touch, but distractingly reminiscent of the silhouette of the hero of the old radio serial *The Shadow*.

The Dutchman has used his immense wealth to persuade Daland to betroth him to Senta. Although the Dutchman can be saved only by a woman who loves him and remains faithful until death, in his desperation, he in effect purchases a bride he has never seen in a loveless arranged marriage. It seems self-defeating, but this kind of delusional thinking is depressingly common among men when it comes to matters of the heart. Fortunately for the Dutchman, Senta already loves him from hearing his tale as a child. Senta, too, is a lonely soul, and she feels immense compassion for the Dutchman. It is a perfect match.

Two more blunders occur in Act III. The act begins with some brilliant choral singing. The setting is the wharf along which Daland's and the Dutchman's ships are anchored. A feast is underway to celebrate the return of Daland's men. Daland's crew and their girlfriends call out to the Dutchman's crew, inviting them ashore and playfully taunting them. There is no reply, so they turn their attention to the feast. But then the Dutchman's ghostly crew begins singing, startling Daland's crew, who try to down them out with their own singing then flee in terror.

The effect of the battling choruses was stunning, but in Lehnhoff's production we do not see two ships by a wharf, but a vast steel box with a barbeque grill in the middle, around which Daland's crew dance, decked out with top hats and canes. When they address the Dutchman's crew, they face the audience. When they cried "Wacht doch auf!" ("Wake up there!") it seemed they were addressing the audience! (I had heard some snoring a few rows behind me.) The Dutchman's sailors were not located on stage. Instead, what appeared to be a pre-recorded tape was blasted out from speakers around the auditorium. A spectacular effect, but not exactly live music. Then there was a lot of running around and banging into things, the clatter of canes hitting the stage, the house lights rising and falling. Then, in the middle of the stage, I saw a mass of huddled men, all of them with bald heads and greenish skin. Was it the Dutchman's ghostly crew? Was it an Uncle Fester look-alike contest? No. These were Daland's Norwegian sailors! What idiocy.

Lehnhoff, however, saved his worst desecration for the very end. When the Dutchman arrived on the scene, Senta was already being courted by Erik, a hunter. Erik would be a good catch for most women, but he seemed utterly ordinary to Senta, who wanted to hold out for a true soul mate—and for a transcendent rather than an earthly sort of love. Once the Dutchman appeared, Erik was completely out of the running. But he came to Senta to plead his case one last time.

Erik's pleas were utterly in vain. But the Dutchman walked in on Senta and Erik and mistakenly concluded that she was being untrue to him. He probably leaped to this conclusion because he had been betrayed by countless other women. These disappointments would naturally cause him to doubt the fairer sex and, what is worse, his own worthiness to be loved. The Dutchman denounces Senta, breaks their engagement, and leaves.

In Lehnoff's production he simply walks back through the doorway through which he first entered. Senta then declares that she will be true to him until death and follows him off stage. Then the whole house goes dark. As far I knew, Senta and the Dutchman eloped together on his ship. Where was the tragedy in that? It seemed rather anticlimactic, almost . . . happy. In short, a real let-down.

As I left the opera house, a friend who had seen a more traditional production told me the real ending. The Dutchman returns to his ship and begins to sail away. Senta, to prove that she was faithful and to deliver the Dutchman from his curse by remaining faithful until death, kills herself by jumping into the sea. The Dutchman's ship then sinks, and the ghostly forms of Senta and the Dutchman rise from the waves embracing. (This last gesture seems to be the kind of concession to Christian sensibilities that turned Nietzsche against Wagner.)

I wondered if Lehnhoff was some sort of first-timer or amateur, an egomaniacal boy genius who was in over his head and who would likely never work again after this travesty. I wondered if he was an envious mediocrity who, not content merely to realize a greater man's work on stage, wished to surpass him, but, unable to do that, was content to vandalize his work instead. I wondered why the Maestro, Donald Runnicles, who had made his reputation as a Wagner conductor, allowed the production to go forward.

It turns out, though, that Nikolaus Lehnhoff is no mere amateur. He has made a career out of desecrating Wagner, which is something of an industry in post-World War II Germany. In 1987 Lehnhoff directed a *Ring* cycle in Munich known as the "spaceship Ring." In 1973, Lehnhoff directed a surrealistic *Tristan und Isolde* in the Roman amphitheater in Orange complete with "trippy" psychedelic lighting effects.

Lehnoff's mentor was none other than Wieland Wagner, the composer's grandson, who from 1951 until his death in 1966, directed a number of Wagner's operas at the family's theater in Bayreuth and elsewhere. Wieland's goal was to strip his grandfather's operas of everything Germanic and Nordic. This was a tall order, since all ten of Wagner's mature operas are based on myths, romances, and folktales from Northern Europe. Not to mention the fact that they were written in German. These elements could not be changed without destroying the works themselves.

But Wieland felt he could get away with changing traditional stagings and costumes, for there has always been some creative leeway in staging operas, even though Wagner himself had very definite ideas about how his operas should be staged, and these ideas were developed after his death, primarily by his widow

Cosima, into what has become the archetypal Wagner style of winged helmets and romantic, fairytale backdrops.

Wieland's "New Bayreuth" was characterized by virtually empty stages. Sets were suggested and spaces demarcated by color and lighting effects. Costumes were "abstract," "modernistic," or "futuristic"—anything but Germanic or Nordic. New Bayreuth was for music what the "international style" was for architecture: cold, clinical, inhumanly drab, and stripped of everything national, historical, or ethnic. In the words of Peter Jonas of the Bavarian State Opera, who approved of New Bayreuth, Wieland "took those myths and purged them of ideology and of the Nordic dream of identity and produced a theater of abstraction, of absolute integrity." (Absolute betrayal is more like it.)

But why? During and after World War II, Richard Wagner and his family were targets of especially intense hatred from the Allies and, behind them, the Jews. Wagner was a German nationalist, a racist, a pagan, and an anti-Semite. Adolf Hitler was deeply influenced by Wagner's music and ideas. Hitler claimed that when he was a teenager, he was first inspired to pursue a political career by Wagner's early opera *Rienzi*.

During his struggle for power, Hitler became friends with Houston Stewart Chamberlain and Winifred Wagner. Chamberlain was the husband of Wagner's daughter Eva and the author of *Foundations of the Nineteenth Century*, an interpretation of the history of the West in terms of the struggles between the Aryan and Jewish races. This book was deeply influenced by Wagner and in turn influenced Hitler's racial interpretation of history and culture.

Winifred was the wife of Wagner's son Siegfried, with whom she had four children, one of them being Wieland. When Siegfried died in 1930, Hitler became something of a surrogate father for Winifred's children, who called him "Uncle Wolf." Hitler and Winifred were such close friends that there were rumors of marriage plans. Hitler even secured an exemption from military service for Wieland during World War II.

Wieland Wagner was apparently one of those histrionic, self-hating, post-war Germans whose weak sense of self-worth had been totally crushed by relentless propaganda about German atrocities, real and fictitious, and German collective guilt for them. After the war, anti-German ethnic cleansing was Allied policy. This was accomplished not just by the expulsion of 14 million Germans from their homes in the East, not just by killing leading German nationalists and purging of millions of their followers from positions of power and influence, but also by the suppression of German identity and nationalist sentiments in all realms of culture. The New Bayreuth style was of a piece with this policy. Perhaps Wieland thought he could redeem and ingratiate himself in the eyes of Germany's new masters by ethnically cleansing his grandfather's works. Lehnhoff, who is German as well, not a Jew, is carrying on the same program.

But there is no appeasing Jewish hatred. Jews can hold a grudge longer than any nation in history. To this day, there is an unofficial but very real ban on performing Wagner's works in Israel. Although Wagner's music has been advocated by many Jewish conductors, including George Solti, James Levine, and Daniel Barenboim, they defend his operas on musical grounds and for what is "universal" in their stories. As one would expect, given Jewish domination of the media, the arts, and the recording industry, the public is not allowed to hear voices that praise Wagner for what is particular about his operas—what is Germanic, what is Nordic.

I don't doubt that Wagner's operas have universal appeal and significance. Anyone can hum a tune and follow a story. But for some there is more to Wagner than just that. As a friend once said, "Mozart and Puccini are art; Wagner is religion." Wagner is a religious experience because something deep in his music connects with something deep in certain listeners, something that has to do with what is particular to Nordic people.

C. S. Lewis once described how, when reading the Norse myths, the words "Baldur the beautiful is dead, is dead," suddenly awakened deep racial memories or archetypes of the ice-clad wastes in which the White race, or at least its Nordic sub-race, probably evolved. Wagner has the same effect. He stirs something in the blood, and he will continue to do so as long as his music and our race survive, no matter how badly his operas are parodied on the stage.

In the long run, Wieland Wagner and Nikolaus Lehnhoff and their kind will be forgotten. In the meantime, is easy enough to avoid such travesties. There are CDs, DVDs, and no shortage of traditional productions. One can even enjoy Lehnhoff's *Dutchman* if one knows the story in advance and is forewarned about the worst bits. When I found the production too distracting, it was easy enough to sweep it all away. All I did was close my eyes. Then there was just Wagner's music, in all its undimmed glory.

December 23, 2004

NADER INSPIRES HOPE

As the debate over the Florida recount continues, I can't help but think it's like a choice between a rotten apple and a rotten orange. Like many other US citizens, I didn't feel comfortable voting for either Vice President Al Gore or Texas Governor George W. Bush.

I chose not to vote this election, but had someone required me to select one of the candidates, I most likely would have chosen Ralph Nader, the consumer advocate.

I would have selected him not because I favor all of the positions he represented, but because he was an honest and forthright candidate, and he was the only third-party candidate who stood a reasonable chance of receiving a sizable percentage of the vote.

My selection might be surprising, since my opinions on certain issues are strongly associated with right-wing ideology. Yet on other matters, such as abortion and environmental issues, many left-wing candidates better represent my views than their right-wing counterparts. Basically, I hate groupthink, be it of the left-wing or the right-wing variety.

The herd mentality of the Christian Right on issues like abortion and the teaching of evolution upsets me just as much as the herd mentality to which many pseudo-intellectual liberals resort whenever politically incorrect subjects are broached.

In both circumstances, group members just know that they're right, rely on strength in numbers to defend their claims, and aren't susceptible to persuasion through reason (though they sometimes pretend to have weighed both sides of an issue).

Additionally, I share Nader's view that special and corporate interests have corrupted politics. The idea that many of our politicians have sold out sickens me. I'm not going to voluntarily cast my vote for a candidate who will, if elected, kneel down and lick the hands—or any other body parts—of whomever contributed the most to his or her election campaign.

On a related note, I can't stand dishonesty and deception coming from any politician, which is why I despise former US Rep. Newt Gingrich ('67C, R-Georgia) just as much as I do US

President Bill Clinton.

I'd much rather have an honest and sincere president with whom I strongly but respectfully disagree, like former US President Jimmy Carter, than a president who shares my views but is a liar with no sense of personal integrity. It speaks volumes that the Republican Party tolerates men like Gingrich, and that the Democratic Party tolerates men like Clinton.

In short, an honest, independent thinker earns my respect much more readily than does someone who simply spouts out the most popular answer to an issue, regardless of which side I take.

For example, Nader, in contrast to both Bush and Gore, has expressed the opinion that the Israelis might bear a much greater burden of responsibility than the Palestinians for starting the latest outbreak of violence in the Middle East. Personal opinions aside, I think nearly everyone can agree that any American political candidate who sympathizes with the Palestinian cause isn't doing so because they believe it will get them more votes.

In the long run, I'm convinced that whether Al Gore or George W. Bush becomes our next president doesn't matter much. Why?

For reasons beyond the scope of this column, the American mainstream has been moving continually farther to the left since the 1960s, and the results of the current election aren't going to stop this trend or alter the *Zeitgeist* of this materialistic, individualistic era in American society.

We'll need a national catastrophe to occur before enough people realize that more exists to national well-being than economic prosperity. In the meantime, all we can hope for is that the people we elect to public office have some shred of honesty and a vision to guide them.

Men who bicker about who will better protect social security or offer better prescription drug benefits for the elderly or who will offer the middle-class the best tax cut are simply saying whatever they need to say in order to get the most votes. But they're not getting mine.

I refer to it as the "Read My Lips factor," and I suspect it's hereditary.

November 17, 2000

September 11th Warrants
Reflection, then Retaliation

This is the final column I wrote for **The Emory Wheel***. I submitted it on September 15, 2001. It was rejected without comment and never appeared in print. School administrators also shut down an online discussion board on which the events of 9/11 were being discussed, saying the board was too "divisive" for the community. Not too surprising, considering Emory's student body is 33% Jewish.*

During the past week, all Americans have had to endure the shock and agony of the most spectacular and deadly terrorist attack in our history. The physical and psychological effects of this attack must be fought with every ounce of American resolve. And those who committed it must be punished swiftly, severely, and to the fullest extent of the law. Under no circumstances must those who resort to killing civilians for the sake of political gain be allowed to escape justice.

On this issue, Americans stand united in the greatest show of support for their country since World War II.

Yet, I remain apprehensive about the next few weeks. My fear is not that America will fail in identifying and bringing to justice the perpetrators of this attack; this nation has repeatedly proven that it is unstoppable when it unites in a common cause. My fear is that the "quiet, unyielding anger" of the American public which President Bush described in his Tuesday address will grow into the fury of a mob. My fear is that US retaliation will, like the original attack, result in excessive loss of innocent life. My fear is that, after everything is said and done, greater anger, misunderstanding, and mistrust will exist between America and the Muslim world than exists right now.

Assuming Osama bin Laden is the culprit, I suggest the following plan of action: (1) Obtain good intelligence on the whereabouts of his terrorist camps in Afghanistan, (2) Send in the most elite of our Special Forces to conduct a surgical strike, (3)

Capture and evacuate bin Laden for a public trial in the US. If America bombs Kabul, attempts to overthrow the Taliban government, or is in any other way overzealous in flexing its military might in the region, we will lose in the long run. We will almost certainly lose the support of the Muslim world, we will jeopardize the support of Russia, and the sympathy felt by millions worldwide for our country's suffering will disappear overnight.

After all, despite what politicians and journalists may say, the attackers were not "cowards." The terrorists committed indescribably horrible and ruthless acts against the American people, but sacrificing one's own life for a cause in which one firmly believes is not cowardice, regardless of how misguided one is. What's tragic about the next few weeks is that, if we use more force than justice requires, good Americans who firmly believe in the cause of protecting the US from terrorism will end up fighting against good Muslims who will only be defending their land. After these Muslims are crushed by the US military, they will be more inclined to consider terrorism as the only way to call attention to the injustices occurring in Palestine. Anger begets anger, and regardless of how much money we spend on anti-terrorist measures, the ugly cycle will repeat itself. What's happening right now in Palestine is an example of such a cycle.

I fear for the next few weeks because of the irresponsible reporting I've already seen on television. The Palestinians who allegedly "danced in the streets and passed out candy" after the attacks were a very small minority. Very little media attention was given to the fact that the attack was condemned by every single Palestinian organization and entity, including Fatah, the Democratic Front for the Liberation of Palestine, the Popular Front for the Liberation of Palestine, and Hamas; Palestinian lawmaker Hanan Ashrawi told a news conference the celebrations were "misguided" and "aberrations" motivated by a feeling among Palestinians that they have been victims of US backing for Israel.

Few know that the US Consul in Jerusalem reported that he has received a huge stack of faxes from Palestinians and Palestinian organizations expressing condolences, grief, and solidari-

ty, or that dozens of Palestinian men, women and, children gathered spontaneously upon hearing the news in front of the US
Consulate in East Jerusalem, lighting candles and placing flow-
ers along its walls. Some of the placards they carried read: "Terror is our common enemy" and "We are victims too."

"We are victims too."

How true that statement is: If only we Americans knew, as
the Palestinians know, what it is like to lose control over one's
own land. If only we knew what it is like to be legally discriminated against, to appeal to the international community and to
be ignored. If only we knew what it is like to have stones returned with bullets, or to endure state-sanctioned torture. If only
Americans knew what it was like to be totally powerless and at
the mercy of another nation . . . and to have the United States,
the most powerful country in the world, provide economic and
military aid to that nation—at a rate of nearly $10 million per
day every day of the year—while at the same time the US piously lectures the rest of the world about human rights abuses. If
Americans understood these things, I might feel more confident
that the US counterattack wouldn't involve any more loss of life
than justice requires.

Responsible Americans should recognize that US foreign policy in the Middle East is partially to blame for the atrocities that
occurred last Tuesday. I would personally like to see the US
adopt a neutral foreign policy in the Middle East. Besides reduc-
ing the threat of anti-US terrorism, such a stance would also help
bring peace to the region. If Israel could no longer count on US
military and economic aid, Jews would be far more inclined to
come to a fair, equitable settlement with the Palestinians.

In any case, an overzealous, iron-fisted American response to
the recent attacks is not the answer: Israel has been responding
to terrorism in such a manner for many years, often killing many
more in counterattacks than were killed in the original attack,
and they still have a problem with terrorism, despite high levels
of security.

I'm betting that the average American hasn't given much
thought to US foreign policy in the Middle East, opting not to
concern himself with an area of the world that doesn't affect him

directly. I'm hoping that the atrocious events of last week cause the average American to give some thought to the policy we want our government to have in the Middle East, instead of merely eliciting a knee-jerk "bomb the hell out of 'em so I can forget about it and go back to watching the game" reaction. For the sake of those who will be targeted if another attack occurs, let's hope for the former.

September 15, 2001

STUDENTS FOR PROPOSITION 54

On September 23, 2003, University of California Regent Ward Connerly addressed Cal. Berkeley students regarding Proposition 54, his "Racial Privacy" ballot initiative. Connerly referred to racial categorization on government forms as a "cruel, arcane system" designed to maintain the *status quo* and expressed his desire for society to question the validity of racial classification. "If you believe in a color-blind ideal," he said, "government ought not to be involved [in racial categorization]."

Aside from a few *ad hominem* emotional outbursts, the question-and-answer session following Connerly's address provided a decent overview of the popular arguments for and against the initiative. Much ink has been spilt detailing the strengths and shortcomings of the initiative.

Proponents tout the measure as a stepping stone towards a color-blind society, saying that the government should not and can not discriminate based on race, it shouldn't collect racial data.

They also note that the measure allows exceptions to this rule whenever there's a "compelling interest" for the state, such as in addressing diseases and other health disparities that afflict one ethnic group more than another.

Opponents of the measure, on the other hand, argue that forbidding the government to collect racial data will hamper its ability to measure and document disparities in education and employment. Arguing in this vein, one impassioned opponent went so far as to suggest that Connerly was implicitly supporting segregation and "white racism" through the measure.

California voters outlawed the consideration of race in college admissions through the passage of Proposition 209. However, admissions officers still may view an applicant's race on the application form, inviting them to discriminate against so-called "overrepresented" White and Asian students in favor of "underrepresented" Black and Hispanic students, all in the name of "equality" and "diversity." Thus Proposition 54 is needed to ensure a truly colorblind admissions process.

Of course, nothing in either Proposition 209 or Proposition 54 prevents admissions officers from taking other considerations into account besides the prospective student's academic merit; although academic criteria (standardized test scores, class rank, and so forth) should take precedence, economic hardships, extracurricular involvement, community service, and so forth can also factor into the equation.

The argument taken by groups such as BAMN (the "Coalition to Defend Affirmative Action and Integration and Fight for Equality By Any Means Necessary"; apparently only the last four words are important enough to include in their acronym) is that any "underrepresentation" of certain racial groups (Blacks and Hispanics) in education is *prima facie* evidence of racism and discrimination at work. However, this argument is flawed because its underlying premise; namely, that racial groups differ in achievement due to environmental variables alone, is belied by the available scientific evidence.

It's a bitter pill to swallow, but performance disparities will *always* exist between racial groups, *because racial groups differ not only due to environmental factors, which can be changed, but also due to genetic factors, which cannot.*

Almost 35 years ago, U.C. Berkeley Professor of Psychology Arthur Jensen (now Emeritus) published an article in the *Harvard Educational Review* entitled "How Much Can We Boost IQ and School Achievement?"[1] Jensen concluded: (1) IQ tests measure socially relevant general ability; (2) individual differences in IQ have a high *heritability* (a measure of the amount of observable variation in a trait attributable to genetic variation in a population), at least for the White populations of the US and Europe; (3) compensatory educational programs have proven generally ineffective in raising the IQs or school achievement of individuals or groups; (4) because social mobility is linked to ability, social class differences in IQ probably have an appreciable genetic component; and tentatively, but most controversially (5) the mean Black-White group difference in IQ probably has some genetic component.

---

[1] A. R. Jensen, "How much can we boost IQ and scholastic achievement?" *Harvard Educational Review*, 39 (1969): 1–123.

Since 1969, Jensen has continued to publish prolifically on all of these issues, and increasing numbers of differential psychologists, psychometricians, and behavioral geneticists have come to agree with one or more of the above conclusions. A questionnaire asked of 661 experts in these fields found that 45% were of the opinion that the Black-White difference in IQ "is a product of both genetic and environmental variation," while only 15% felt that the difference stemmed from environmental variables alone.[2] A statement[3] by 52 experts on intelligence published in the *Wall Street Journal* holds that "IQ is strongly related, perhaps more so than any other single measurable human trait, to many important educational, occupational, economic, and social outcomes," that "intelligence tests are not culturally biased against American blacks or other native-born, English-speaking peoples in the US," and that "the [IQ] bell curve for whites is centered roughly around 100; for American blacks around 85; and those for different subgroups of Hispanics roughly midway between those for whites and blacks." *The Bell Curve*[4] contains an original analysis of 11,878 youths (including 3,022 Blacks) from the 12-year National Longitudinal Survey of Youth. It found that most 17-year-olds with high scores on the Armed Forces Qualification Test (an intelligence test), regardless of ethnic background, went on to occupational success by their late 20s and early 30s, while those with low scores were more inclined to welfare dependency. The study also found that the average IQ for "African" Americans was lower than those for "Latino," "White," "Asian," and "Jewish" Americans (85, 89, 103, 106, and 113, respectively, pp. 273–78).[5]

---

[2] M. Snyderman and S. Rothman, "Survey of expert opinion on intelligence and aptitude testing," *American Psychologist,* 42 (1987): 137–144.

[3] L. Gottfredson, "Mainstream Science on Intelligence," *Wall Street Journal* (December 13, 1994), A18.

[4] R. J. Herrnstein and C. Murray, *The Bell Curve: Intelligence and Class Structure in American Life* (New York: Free Press, 1994).

[5] Interestingly enough, these IQ scores are remarkably in accordance with the 2003 SAT I results of 857 for African-Americans, 912 for Hispanics (averaged from Mexican-Americans, Puerto Ricans, and "other" Hispanics), 1,063 for Whites, and 1,083 for Asians. Source:

Of course, there's not enough room in this flyer to do more than scratch the topic.[6] It's worth noting, however, that Jensen's theories have not been scientifically discredited despite nearly 35 years of vigorous attempts to do so, that Jensen himself is well-respected by his colleagues for both his scientific rigor and personal integrity, and that Jensen has recently received numerous awards and honors[7] for his contributions (which include seven books and over 400 articles published in peer-reviewed scientific journals) to the field of educational psychology. With each passing year, opponents of Jensen must rely on increasingly improbable *ad hoc* hypotheses to explain away the Black-White difference in IQ and SAT scores. Similar, increasingly improbable and

---

http://www.collegeboard.com/prod_downloads/about/news_info/c bsenior/yr2003/pdf/graph10.pdf Not too surprisingly, BAMN decided in 2001 that the SAT test itself is racist (just as they would likely allege IQ tests are, contrary to the opinions of expert psychologists). See http://www.bamn.com/doc/2001/011205-speakout-ucb.htm

[6] Probably the best place to start a comprehensive review of the merits of Arthur Jensen's research is in F. Miele, *Intelligence, Race, and Genetics: Conversations with Arthur R. Jensen* (Boulder, Colo.: Westview Press, 2002). In a book geared towards a lay audience, Miele (who is himself agnostic and extremely skeptical on the issue) asks Jensen a number of pointed questions designed to elucidate his position *vis-à-vis* the positions of his detractors.

[7] In 1998 an issue of the journal *Intelligence* appeared entitled "A King Among Men: Arthur Jensen," containing praise from his colleagues (not all of whom agree with his theories on race differences.) In 2003, Jensen received the Kistler Prize (including a $100,000 cash award and a 180-gram gold medal) from The Foundation for the Future, whose selection committee is made up of prominent members of the academic community. Past recipients include esteemed professors Luigi Luca Cavalli-Sforza, Stanford University (2002); Richard Dawkins, Oxford University (2001); and Edward O. Wilson, Harvard University (2000). Also in 2003 editions of *The Scientific Study of General Intelligence: A Tribute to Arthur R. Jensen* (edited by Helmuth Nyborg, published by Elsevier Science) went to press. According to the publisher, "this book celebrates two triumphs in modern psychology: the successful development and application of a solid measure of general intelligence, and the personal courage and skills of the man who made this possible: Arthur R. Jensen from UC-Berkeley."

unrealistically sophisticated explanations arose to defend the geocentric model of orbital motion prior to its replacement by the heliocentric model.

Assuming Jensen is correct, Black and Hispanic "underrepresentation" *should be expected* at institutions of higher learning that do not discriminate on the basis of race, as well as in public employment for jobs demanding a high level of whatever IQ measures. Likewise, the evidence suggests Asians and Jews should be overrepresented relative to their numbers in the general population.

What does all this mean for Cal students? Although current White and Asian students won't be affected by the defeat of Proposition 54, their younger siblings may well find themselves discriminated against in favor of lesser qualified Black or Hispanic applicants. Furthermore, those who do get admitted will find themselves slowed down by the presence of unqualified students in their classes. This can only lead to an increase in racial tensions.

Connerly envisions a truly "colorblind" society in which people are treated as individuals rather than as members of particular groups. But we have to accept that in such a society, the genetic differences between groups will manifest themselves as differences in achievement which cannot be dismissed as effects of some sort of "institutionalized" or "underground" racism.

September 26, 2003

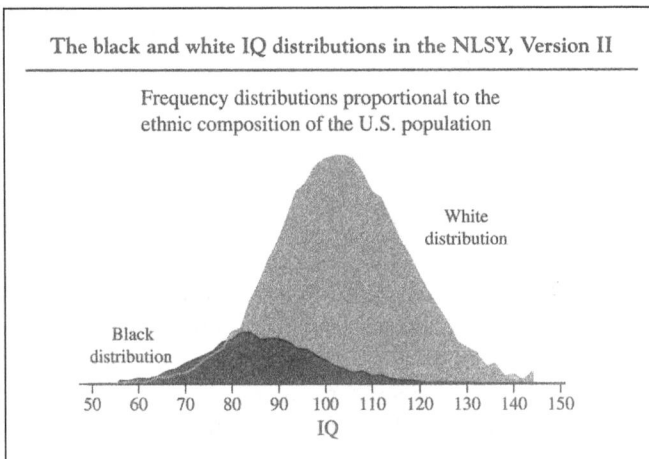

The black and white IQ distributions in the NLSY, Version II

Frequency distributions proportional to the ethnic composition of the U.S. population

VOTE FOR BUSH

In November of 2004, I voted to re-elect George W. Bush, and I urged all Whites to do the same. I was not being facetious. Here are my reasons.

I am not voting for Bush because of his policies, which are anti-White in the extreme. He is squandering White blood and treasure in Iraq to serve not our nation's interests, but the interests of Jews around the world, while he is allowing non-Whites to flood White living spaces, take White jobs, consume White resources, pollute the White gene pool, and further dilute White political control over our destiny as a people.

I am not voting for Bush because of his character. Clearly one of Bush's attractions to the GOP powerbrokers is his lack of good character. He is vain and insecure, so he is easily flattered. He is small-minded and narcissistic, so he is satisfied with the empty trappings of power, leaving the real power in the hands of others. He lacks intelligence and curiosity, so he is easily fooled. He is intellectually lazy and indecisive, so he depends upon his advisors. He is shameless, so he can lie with the appearance of sincerity and betray any person or principle that gets in his way. In short, Bush is the perfect ventriloquist dummy for the corporate oligarchs and court Jews that surround him.

I am not voting for Bush because I think he is the lesser of two evils. He is the greater evil.

I am voting for Bush because I think that Jewish corruption of our culture and political system is the greatest problem White Americans face. Until Jewish power is exposed and broken, none of our other problems can be fixed.

Under the Bush administration, Jewish corruption has never been greater. But since 9/11 and the Iraq war, Jewish power has never been more exposed and vulnerable.

More Americans than ever before have been awakened to the Jewish problem. A few days after 9/11 both NBC and Reuters polled Americans on why it happened. Both polls reported that two thirds of Americans believed that our close alliance with

Israel was to blame. These polls were quickly pulled, and although I have no doubt that Americans continue to be asked this question by pollsters, no results have been released to the public.

More Americans than ever before are speaking out about the Jewish problem, including prominent figures like Ralph Nader, Senator Hollings, and General Zinni. I constantly encounter White Americans of every social class and shade of the political spectrum who will privately discuss the Jewish problem with very little prompting once they feel safe to speak their minds. They do not speak out in public because they feel they are alone. They would speak out if they realized that they were not alone and that others would come to their defense if they were attacked.

Every time a public figure breaks the silence, the Jews are in a no-win situation. If they go on the attack, they expose themselves as bullies, crybabies, and sophists. They also risk having the overused term "anti-Semite" lose its negative connotations — or even become a mark of honor — as more and more mainstream, reasoned, and respected critics are labeled "anti-Semites" for candidly expressing their views. Yet if they remain silent, others are emboldened. Either way, the silent millions watch and learn.

Bush's critics have many motives, from high principle to pure partisanship to personal animosity. But whatever their motives, the more Bush's critics dig into the causes and consequences of 9-11 and the Iraq war, the more evidence of Jewish corruption will come to light.

If Bush is re-elected, this trend will only gain momentum. Perhaps the Jewish media will no longer be able to contain it. Then there will be an unprecedented free and frank national discussion of the Jewish problem. Such a discussion would be the beginning of the end of Jewish power in America.

The loathing of Bush by the Left is almost pathological. The Left had similar antipathy toward Richard Nixon and Ronald Reagan. When they won re-election, the Left went crazy and fought fanatically to bring down both Presidents: Nixon with Watergate, Reagan with Iran-Contra. If Bush is re-elected, he will get the same treatment. If the hatred is intense enough, non-

Jewish Leftists may throw Semitically Correct strictures aside as they close for the kill. And there is little chance that the Bush administration and the Jewish power structure could withstand such scrutiny.

If Kerry is elected, however, the same anti-White policies and Jewish corruption will continue. But the critical momentum toward discussing the Jewish problem will be lost. The neo-conservative Jews will scuttle toward the wainscoting, to be replaced by a new cast of left-wing Jews who will pursue the same policies under different and more subtle disguises. Left-wing criticism of Jewish power will be all but extinguished, and there is little chance that mainstream conservatives will take up the torch. (Even if they did, the momentum would still have been lost.)

In a sane and healthy society, we would study the candidates and vote for the best man. But America is not a sane and healthy society, and things will have to get a lot worse before they can get better. Bush will make things get worse faster and hasten the day when the healing can begin.

That is why it is imperative that we re-elect George W. Bush.

October 30, 2004

ABOUT THE AUTHOR

MICHAEL J. POLIGNANO was born in 1980 in Frederick, Maryland. He first came to national attention in 2000 when, as an undergraduate at Emory University, he ignited a storm of controversy by writing in the school newspaper about the scientifically established fact that racial differences are largely genetic. He graduated from Emory in 2002. He is a writer, publisher, activist, and information technology consultant based in San Francisco. This is his first book.

www.ingramcontent.com/pod-product-compliance
Lightning Source LLC
Chambersburg PA
CBHW051725260326
41914CB00031B/1745/J